THE BAR REST

GUIDE TO DOUBLING YOUR PROFITS & LOYAL REGULARS IN ANY ECONOMY

Your Step-by-Step Blueprint for Attracting New Customers & Turning Them into Loyal Regulars

The Bar Restaurant Owner's Guide to Doubling Your Profits & Loyal Regulars in Any Economy

Your Step-by-Step Blue Print for Attracting New Customers & Turning Them into Loyal Regulars

by

Nick Fosberg

ISBN 978-1-105-55147-5

There is only one person I can dedicate this book to: my father.
If not for him, I wouldn't have written it or be where I am today.

Introduction

If you are like most bar or restaurant owners, you're not completely happy with the money you are making or the hours you are spending running your place of business. Being able to attract paying customers is not as easy as it once was. Before all you had to do was put out a few ads on the radio or in the newspaper, and you had customers walking in your doors. Not anymore!

Competition is at an all-time high. Customers now have more choices then they can imagine: sports bars, karaoke bars, lounges, nightclubs, restaurants, etc. Every bar or restaurant now attracts certain groups of people who have specific needs and wants. **This book is going to present a radical prescription for change in the way you attract exactly who you want and how you will keep them coming back to spend more money.**

Let me introduce myself. My name is Nick Fosberg, I own Casey's Pub in Loves Park, Illinois, and I'm the president and founder of Bar Owner Marketing Systems. My dad has been in the bar business for the last thirty-five years, and when I was twenty-four, he sold me one of his bars. Then things got interesting. Because I'd grown up in the business I thought I knew everything, but I was wrong. I didn't know a shit about marketing or how to attract new customers—at least, not in a cost-effective way.

After one year, I was very close to going out of business due to the economy and to new competition in the area. Every day I heard my regulars telling me they'd lost their jobs, they were going into foreclosure, their hours got cut, they couldn't find a job. People were scared to spend a penny! Suddenly I found myself paying bills out of my own pocket to keep the place running. This was my wake-up call—*and it's the best thing that ever happened to me.*

I knew marketing was the only thing that could bring my bar back to life without discounting. I researched on the Internet, bought marketing courses, went to marketing seminars, hired marketing experts to work with one-on-one. I became so intrigued by what I was learning I became a direct-marketing junkie!

After just three months of working with these experts, I started to implement what they told me to do. It was tough at first because what they taught me was a kind of like a foreign language, but it worked. I slowly saw a positive response from my marketing, new customers coming in the doors, and repeat visits.

Then one day I hit a gold mine. One of my mentors said, **"What can you do that makes you the most money in the shortest amount of time?"** It took me a while to answer this, but then that light bulb went off. The answer was *parties.*

I remembered that when someone had a party or event at my bar it brought in forty to sixty people on average, most of them where new customers, and they drank like fish! So we decided to write a letter and send it out to three hundred businesses in my area for office holiday parties with an offer that was almost too good to be true.

Within two days I had booked thirteen parties, and each party had a minimum of fifty people. This brought in over eight hundred people and only cost me around three hundred dollars. The average check for each person was close to twenty dollars—that's *sixteen thousand dollars* in sales from a three-hundred-dollar investment. To be exact, it was $16,091!

That's when I realized this is where the money is. I needed to get groups of people into my bar. So over the next several months, I tried different marketing strategies to book events and parties and finally created a proven system to get groups of fifty to seventy-five people in my doors two to four times every single week, even during the traditional slow times of the year, without spending a dime on advertising. My sales doubled; I quit using radio, TV, and newspaper advertising as my main source of advertising, which saved me about two thousand dollars a month; and I was bringing hundreds of new faces into my bar every month.

My next big breakthrough was using my business to help pay people's medical bills due to sudden illnesses. I figured out a way that I could help people in need and still make a profit in the long run for myself. This is a very powerful way to do business and get great respect from your community. As soon as the media heard what I was doing, I was bombarded with phone calls from my local media stations to get the story. Within three days I had received over thirty thousand dollars in prime-time exposure over a two-week period and booked five to seven benefits. This didn't cost me one dime and it brought in five to seven hundred new faces into my bar. I don't go into this in my book, but you can see these write-ups at www.BarOwnerMarketingSystems.com or www.RockfordSupport.com

After doubling my sales within eight months, I realized I had something extremely unique and profitable that nobody else in my area or industry was doing. I've now started Bar Owner Marketing Systems to help bar owners outside my area increase their sales, decrease their marketing costs, and take care of 90 percent of their most important job, marketing. My goal for each bar is to put more money in their pockets with very little effort and apply just a small change to the way they market their business. There isn't anything I'd rather do than share my knowledge and expertise with other bar owners and help them increase their business with less effort and more time off. I love the bar business and I love helping people succeed.

It's ultimately about **how we market our business, how we communicate with our customers, and what we can offer our existing customers and new customers that our competition isn't offering.** Each bar owner needs to give people a reason to come to his or her bar over any other bar.

To this day I continue to spend twenty-five thousand dollars or more per year to further my education by staying in coaching programs, going to marketing seminars, and buying marketing courses. I learn something new every month that makes me more money, makes my life easier, or gives me the upper hand against my competition—and I firmly believe that having a coach or mentor is one of the smartest things any entrepreneur can do in any business. Every athlete has coaches, the president has advisors, famous actors have acting coaches...why? *Nobody knows everything and nobody is perfect!*

I hope this book will open your eyes to how you should be marketing your business. What you are about to discover will get you positive results extremely fast, and you see profits increase rapidly with very little investment.

So sit down, close the door, drink a Red Bull, and let this work on your brain. This will be one of the most important things you read all year, and I hope it changes your life like it did mine.

> "You can have everything you want in life if you will just help enough other people get what they want."
>
> —Zig Ziglar

Find out what your customers want and give it to them!

Your Marketing and Advertising Makeover Is Finally Here

Most bar owners' strategy for advertising and marketing is horrible. I can't tell you how much time and money are wasted and how many opportunities are lost. Most bar owners are clueless as to the difference between good and bad marketing.

This book is going to present you with an opportunity to make a small change in your marketing. If you do, you will make more money, cut your marketing costs in half, and never have to worry about your competition or a slow economy.

When you're finished with this book you will never look at an ad the same! Your advertising is going to be completely different than your competitors', and when they see your ads and marketing they will probably think you are a fool. *This is what you want.* You will just ignore all this and keep doing what you are doing because results are all that matters when it comes to marketing. Who cares what your ads look like as long as you are making a big profit from them?

I get paid thousands of dollars to create and write marketing campaigns for private clients. I don't tell you this to brag. I'm telling you this to impress you with the extremely high value of the book you are starting to read. Master the steps in this book, and I promise your life and income will change.

Contents

CHAPTER 1

Why the Old-school Approach Is Now Obsolete

If you are like 95 percent of bar and restaurant owners, you are either shoveling money into marketing but not getting a return on your investment or you've quit spending money on marketing because you feel it is a waste. Bar owners are advertising victims; they are preyed upon by media salespeople and ad agencies. In all honesty, these people don't know shit about marketing, the bar business, or how to make a sale. The only thing they know how to sell is space! But most bar owners copy what they see their competition or larger chains doing, and that is *traditional advertising.*

Traditional advertising is all about branding. It's about your logo in large print on the headline of an ad, the special you are promoting, and your address and phone number—that's it.

Think about the ads that you have done; think about the ones sales reps have done for you. Open your newspaper today and look at your competition's ads. Listen to the radio. I guarantee most of what you see or hear is a single special or event being promote—but they don't make an offer! *$6.95 Fish Fry This Friday…$3 You-Call-Its…*Who the hell cares! And how do you track your marketing with this kind of ad? If you want to know where the best bang for your buck is, you must give your customers a reason to respond and be able to track where every single customer is coming from. Sounds hard, right? It's easy, and I'll get to that shortly.

When you use traditional advertising or mass advertising, you are using what I call the shotgun approach. You are trying to hit every damn person you can. You want as many people to see your advertising as possible, right? Wrong! Think about it like this: when you use traditional advertising, you are hitting people from half a mile to thirty or more miles away. We are in the bar business. How many people who live twenty miles away do you really think are going to come to your bar? Very few!

What you want to use is *direct marketing*, which I call the rifle approach. You want to target exactly who you want in your bar—the people who are the most likely to respond to your offer. Doesn't it make more sense to go after a thousand targeted people rather than ten thousand people who are highly unlikely to come in?

Today's customers have more options then they ever have. Non-targeted advertising is a waste of money. Instead, market to the people who are likely to respond. And if you are not marketing at all, you are setting yourself up for disaster. Marketing is the only way to bring in new customers, and every business needs a consistent flow of new customers to stay alive.

CHAPTER 2

The Direct Marketing Difference

Direct marketing is salesmanship in print in some sort of media that quickly provides you with results. Let me explain some rules that you *must* follow with every single ad no matter what kind of media you choose. If you don't follow these rules, you might as well give your money to your competitors.

1. There will always be an offer or offers.
2. You will give customers clear instructions on how to respond.
3. You will get them to respond right now!
4. There will always be an expiration date.
5. There will be tracking and measurement on everything you do.
6. There will be follow up-and there will be strong sales copy.
7. Your marketing will not look like traditional advertising.

Let me explain some of these rules to you so you understand them more clearly.

#1 There Will Always Be an Offer

No matter what, there is always going to be an offer at your bar. Direct marketing is designed to make you a profit *now*, and if you don't have an offer, how the hell are you going to get customers in your bar?

What's in it for me? This is how you, me, and everyone else think when we are approached with an ad, offer, or anything. When your sales rep comes in with a new flavored vodka but you don't have any room because you have twenty-five other flavored vodkas (that probably taste just the same), you ask, "Why should I add this? What kind of deal are you going to give me? How much more will I make with this vodka than the others?"

The better the offer the better the response you will get. One or two dollars off won't get you far. Don't be cheap! The more you give, the more you will receive. If you want more new customers or old customers to come in and come back, make them a great offer, plain and simple!

You must always have some type of expiration or limited quantity in your marketing. This is what puts money in your cash register **NOW** and this is a great way to make sure your offer gets used.

#2 You Will Give Customers Clear Instructions on How to Respond

People are usually pretty good at following directions, but if you confuse them you will lose them as prospects. Give them simple, easy ways to respond. Tell them how they can get your discounted offer; guide them to what you want them to do next.

If you are sending out a postcard, tell customers to bring it in to get the discount. If you are sending out a letter, tell them to call you and when is the best time, or to e-mail you and give you their contact information.

You need to talk to potential customers and existing customers as if they are your children. Trust me! Keep it simple, stupid, so they understand how to get the great value you are offering.

You might be thinking, *Why would I want to tell them how to respond?* **How else are you going to track your marketing and see if it's working or not?**

#3 You Will Get Them to Respond Right Now!

#4 There Will Always Be an Expiration Date

Like I said before, direct marketing is designed to make you a profit right away. We want money in your pockets this week, not next month!

How are you going to get them to respond now? Put an expiration date in your ad, or make it limited to only X amount of people. **Your goal is to get people off their lazy asses before it's too late**. Create some urgency!

I'm sure you know what I mean about an expiration date: *offer valid until 5/31, expires 5/31*, etc. But let's say you want to pick up a slow weeknight by offering a free meal. You can say, "First fifty people in the door after five p.m. will get a free meal up to $6.95" or "Only available this week or Tuesday."

If you don't have some type of a limited time or amount of something, your potential customer won't act on it and will probably forget about your offer. Everyone procrastinates! Get them in your doors right away.

Remember the sixteen-thousand-dollar sales letter I told you about? This had everything to do with urgency. I sent out this sales letter to around three hundred businesses in my area and offered them a great deal on a party package during the holidays. What made this so successful was that I was only giving this away to the first ten businesses that called and responded.

I got calls the next day after putting these in the mail, and every single person said, "Am I one of the first ten people?" or "Am I too late?" The truth is, I would have booked all three hundred if they all called, but they didn't know that. They thought only ten people were getting it, and they also felt like this was a really great deal since I was only giving ten away. If I was offering it to anyone and everyone, this offer wouldn't be as valuable.

> If you are interested in getting this sales letter or a similar sales letter written for you, this is part of my area-exclusive coaching program. You can get more information at the end of this book about how to get on the waiting list.

You must always have some type of expiration or limited quantity in your marketing. This is what puts money in your cash register *now*, and it is a great way to make sure your offer gets used.

#5 There Will Be Tracking and Measurement on Everything You Do

There must be a way to track every ad. If you're guessing like all the others on what's working, **you're losing money**. How will you know if you are getting a good return on your investment if you don't know how much money you are making on your ads? Track, track, track...This is very important!

How do you track and measure your marketing? Every month I send out a "rip card," which is a postcard with a business-card-sized tear-off on the end. That tear-off is a $7.50 gift card, and when customers use it I have my staff staple it to the receipt so I can see how much more money they spent. At the end of the month, I add up the total additional sales and see how much money these brought in over the price of what I paid to send them out.

You can do tracking for every ad you send—just like the example I gave you about the sales letter. I knew what it cost me to mail, I was able to track how well it performed because people who received it had to call me, and I checked the average sales that each party brought in.

You can tell customers to cut out a coupon or certificate and bring it in, or tell them to mention the ad to get your offer, etc. Another great way to track your marketing is by using the Internet and a simple one-page Web site. Send people to a site to get a free gift card, and require that they input their information on the site. You can include a little box that asks where they heard about the site. This way you can see exactly what is bringing you results.

#5 There Will Be Follow-Up and There Will Be Strong Sales Copy

This is one of the biggest mistakes I made in the business. If I were to bet, I'd say 99 percent of bar owners do not follow up with their customers. You might even be asking yourself, "What do you mean, follow up with them?"

Once you see your ads are working and new customers are coming in, you have a very important job that can double your sales within one year! **You need to capture these new customers' information so you can get them back more often.**

What's important for you to understand is that you spent money to get them in the door. They raised their hand and said, "I like your offer and I go to bars." *This is exactly what you want.* You are generating more ideal customers like your loyal regulars, and you need a way to follow up with them to get them back to your bar. How do you do this? Capture their information by running contests for giveaways, or create a loyalty program.

Get a name, address, cell phone, and e-mail at the very least. Once you have all this information, you can send offers to your new clients get them in your doors more often. There are several e-mail, text Services, and direct mail services you can use. I will go more into detail on this later in the book.

You must follow up with new and existing customers every month to remind them why you are better than any other bar in your area.

> If you don't want to go through all the trouble and time of following up with customers, look into my "Done-for-You" marketing program at the end of the book. Wouldn't it be nice to have an automated marketing system that does all the work for you and is guaranteed to bring in profits? No more guesswork or trying to stay organized.

We're not done here. You absolutely must use strong sales copy in your follow-up. Give reasons why you are presenting the offer, tell a story, figure out what frustrates your customers and attack that and explain how you are their solution.

Most of my customers don't like to sit at home, they don't want to cook, they want to be entertained, and the single men want to talk to cute girls behind the bar. **Explain to them in your sales letter, postcard, or**

whatever, that *you* are the solution to the problem they might be facing. Tell them why they need to come to your bar and how you are the solution.

#6 Your Marketing Will Not Look Like Traditional Advertising

As I explained before, traditional ads have a big company logo at the top, a sale price or event, and contact information—maybe with a few graphics.

Your marketing will have a big, bold headline that draws the attention of your readers and makes them read the rest of your ad. Either there will be some kind of coupon or certificate attached to your ad that customers will have to bring in so you can track the ad, or the ad will tell them how to respond to get whatever it is that you are offering.

The only thing that matters in marketing your business is the results. You will be able to know what your results are by using direct marketing. You need to look at your results and see if you are making money or losing money for everything you do.

Yes, at first it does take a little effort and time to get used to tracking the results. It took me about three months to come up with a consistent and organized way. To tell you the truth, I hated doing it, but the results show you what's working. Was my ad worth it? If not, I would do something else. If the ad was successful and I made a bunch of money, then I knew to keep running it.

At first direct marketing seemed like it wouldn't work for my business. The ads looked different, nobody else in the bar business was marketing like this, and it just didn't feel right. This was hard for me to face at first, and it took a little change in the way I ran my business, but it is the smartest and best thing I have ever done.

If you are serious about making more money, having a unique advantage over you competition, and easily turning new customers into loyal regulars, these next chapters are going to be the key to your success.

CHAPTER 3

The Three Keys To Direct Marketing

The most important ingredient you will need to understand before we go on is that you are no longer a bar owner. You are not in the bar business. **You are in the marketing business. You are a marketer of your bar, and that's it.**

Having a successful and profitable bar is not about your specials, your food, your staff, or your entertainment. **It's all about the marketing.** You can have the best specials in town, the most entertaining events, and the best food, but if people don't know about these then how the hell are you going to benefit from them? You need to have an affordable and profitable way to reach new and existing customers to tell them why they need to come to your bar over your competition's.

The most successful bar owners understand this. Your most important and valuable job is marketing. This is what brings money to the register, and the techniques I'm about to teach you are what will set you aside from your competition and give you dominance.

There are three keys to direct marketing. They are market—media—message. These don't go in any order, neither is one more important than the other, but you need all three in place for every marketing plan you create. Think of it as having a three-legged barstool: you won't be able to sit if you are missing one leg, and you won't succeed without all three keys.

The way that these three keys work is that you need to have the right message, going to the right market, with the right media. If you can do this every time, you will have a successful ad that will produce results. Let me explain these three in more detail.

Market

Market equals *who*. Who are you going to market to? **Who are your best customers, who are you trying to attract to your bar, who will respond to your message?** Most bar owners don't even know who they are trying to attract or who will respond. They want everyone, but we all know that everyone doesn't want to come to our bar. We have to select the right people and target that group.

I want you to think of who your best customers are. In most cases these are regulars who come in four to five times a week spending twenty-five to fifty dollars each time they are in. Now I want you think of who they really are: what are their ages, what kind of work do they do, are they single, are they married. When you can define *who* it is you want, it will be easier for you to get more of those people by sending them a message that matches what they want.

I do a lot of marketing by direct mail using postcards. My best customers are my regulars obviously, and they are anywhere from thirty to fifty-five (for the four to eight p.m. crowd), they are single men, and they all live within three-to-five-mile radius of my bar.

To bring in more people like this, I bought a mailing list of exactly that, single males in that age range who lived within that radius of my address, and I sent them an offer they couldn't refuse. Once I got them in the door, we signed them up for our loyalty program, which then allowed me to market directly to them, which brought them in more, and they become regulars. Can you see how powerful this is? I will go more into detail about loyalty programs later.

Let's say you want to do a ladies night. Obviously your target market is women. What age range? You already know people are not driving long distances, right? So buy a mailing list of women within the age range you want and a certain radius of your bar, and deliver them an offer to get them in your bar. Then figure out a way to get the ones who respond to come back more often.

Here is my direct marketing strategy in a nutshell: market to a certain niche of people, offer them something they can't refuse, get them in the door, capture their information by getting them into a drawing or loyalty program, then follow up with them with more marketing by text, e-mail, direct mail, and voice broadcast to get them coming back and turn them into loyal regulars. It's that simple. That's the simple formula you need to double your profits.

Your goal is to find a crowd of people starving for what you have to offer. Most bar owners who advertise spend tons of money and only get a few of those starving people. Wouldn't it be great to market to only the starving crowd?

When you advertise with radio, TV, and newspaper, you are getting your message out to a massive market of people—but how many of those people really care? Maybe 1 percent.

Take the five hundred dollars, or whatever you spend with high-priced advertising, and stick it into direct mail or another way to target a specific group that is more likely to come to your bar. If you choose to use the newspaper, put a flyer in there that only goes to your zip code. *Don't try to hit the whole damn city!*

Target your existing customers.

Fact: It is seven times more profitable to market to your existing customers than it is to someone who has never been to your bar! I will get more into depth about his later in the book. Make sure to check this out because this is where you should be doing 80 to 90 percent of your marketing.

Message

If you don't have a *message* to promote, than you are back to traditional advertising. **Your *message* is going to be your offer, and your offer must match your market.** If the market you are going after is women, then you don't want your message to be about beer and chicken wings! It needs to be a strong message, so offer something for free just to get them in the door or give them 50 percent off on their tab good up to ten dollars off. If you give them a lousy offer, most likely they won't respond.

Remember, all people care about these days is what's in it for them—*why should I come here and not there?* You must give them a reason to come to your bar and then capture their information and market to them over and over. Create some urgency. You want to make money now, not later.

Media

Media is postcards, e-mail, text messages, social media, sales letters, etc. The list can go on and on. What works best? It all depends on what you are offering, who you are targeting, and what you think is the best and most cost-effective way to get your message read.

If you are going after existing customers, I recommend text messaging because everyone in the world has a phone now and everyone reads their messages. I've read that 98 percent of people read every text message they get. The only downfall is that you only have so much room to complete your message.

I've said before not to use TV, newspaper, and radio advertising—but I don't mean never. As long as you are applying direct marketing principles to your ads, it can work for you. But it is expensive, and there are far more, better ways to spend your money.

New Age Media You Need to Be Using

Don't let this scare you if you don't know much about computers and the Internet because there is always someone to hire this out to. I offer Web design and campaign setup, and 75 percent percent of the bar owners I work with don't understand computers or how to use the Internet to increase business. That's why it's my job to take care of this for them.

Facebook Ads: I'm not talking about posting something on Facebook here. I'm talking about paying for advertising on Facebook. If you are familiar with this, great; if not, you need to understand it because you can really target exactly who you want for around fifty cents a person.

Facebook allows you to create small ads that include a picture and make an offer. The great thing about this is that you can choose who sees the ad: men or women or both, in certain zip codes, of certain age ranges. You can even break it down to their interests.

You create the ad, and when they click it, it takes them to a Web page that you direct them to, either your Web site or a one-page site that you create just for your offer.

Google Ads: You can create ads the same exact way you do on Facebook, but this time you'll be on the number-one ranked search engine in the world. This is where everyone is going to find information and search for bars in your area.

There is a little sneaky trick that I will fill you in on. You can create campaigns based on what other people are searching for. People who go to bars in your area probably get on to see your specials, promos, or your competition's specials. The sneaky trick is that you can set up a campaign under your competitor's name. **So if someone looks up ABC Bar (your competition), you can have an ad that comes up right next to them!** You can target people who are looking up your competition and advertise a free gift card or something to get them in your doors.

Become an expert in direct marketing or find someone who is!

I won't go into full detail about internet strategies but I wanted to put this in your head as something to think about. My advice is this: hire someone who is a Google ads expert and have them run your campaigns for you. It will save you time and money. Don't try to do everything yourself. Do what you're good at and hire everything else out.

Marketing is the key to your business. Marketing is what drives customers into our bars. If you want to make a shit load of money, I suggest you read thirty minutes a day about direct marketing, sales, or copywriting. (Copywriting is using salesmanship in print, selling the words in your marketing)

Buy books and courses. Go to seminars. **Marketing is the most profitable and most important job of any bar owner.** If you don't want to read and learn how to be a master marketing expert, then find someone who understands it and let them do your marketing for you.

CHAPTER 4

The Bar Owner's Breakdown

So you're frustrated with your marketing and the amount of money you spend because you're not getting the results you want in your bar. Your advertising sales reps make you huge promises, but at the end of the day you feel you have wasted your money. Am I right? Or are you 100 percent satisfied with the results you get?

At this point most bar owners stop spending money on advertising. They feel it's a waste of money and believe that the only people who are going to come in are their regulars. But this is the wrong attitude. If you want to be successful and have the lifestyle you *really* want, you need new customers walking in your doors every day.

Fear holds a lot of us back. Fear that something won't work. Fear of going broke, Fear of what people will think of us. The most successful entrepreneurs learn to get over this and try new things. *This is going to be one of your biggest challenges, but you must make this happen.*

Don't give up. Think of this book as your survival guide. The reason your marketing isn't working is because either you're not using direct marketing or if you are you are doing something wrong.

If you are sending the right message to the right audience, you will have new customers walking in your doors. If you have the right follow-up system in place to turn these new customers into loyal customers (which I will talk about later), **you will have the ultimate advantage over every bar owner in your area!**

Bar owners have been using the same marketing strategies for years and years. Like I mentioned before, times are changing, the way we communicate with customers is changing, and our customers buying deaccessions are changing. They have more choices than they ever have. Restaurants and bars are all over the place. Competition is at its all-time highest and most competitive.

If you are using the same marketing techniques as your competition or not marketing at all, you'd better think twice, because you're in for a rude awakening. Marketing is the only way to increase your sales. Sitting around blaming the economy is just an excuse, not the answer.

How to Increase Your Sales by 40 Percent in a Matter of Ten Weeks

I had a private coaching client who was ready to give up and shut her doors. She was at the point where she couldn't keep up with rent to pay the landlord. I asked her what she was doing to drive in new customers, and she told me, "Nothing." She felt it was a waste of money because everything she'd tried wasn't working.

I asked her some other questions about her bar so I could get a better idea of the best approach to increase her sales quickly but with the least amount of money. What I discovered was that she had a decent-size place that held about 120 to 140 people, a great menu, and good food, but her competition was kicking her ass.

The only thing that was going to help her fast enough to save her bar was getting large groups of people into her bar to create some big paydays. I designed some different party packages for her, defined her best target market to go after, wrote a sales letter, bought a mailing list, and sent out the letter.

Within one week she had booked nine parties with anywhere from thirty to seventy-five people. She was extremely happy, but I told her not to get too excited yet. This wasn't going to save her bar. She was confused and didn't understand.

I told her the most important thing she needed to do was to capture the information of every single person that walked in her doors during these parties. This way she could try to get them back in within a week or two with an irresistible offer, and get them spending more money.

She was able to capture about 80 percent of the personal contact information of people who came for her parties, and she followed up with them with the same irresistible party package offer that she gave the guests who'd brought everyone in. **Every month after that she has been averaging fifteen parties a month with an average of forty-five people per party and has increased her sales by 40 percent!**

CHAPTER 5

The Essential Parts of a Successful Ad

Now I'm going to go more into depth about what you need in each ad. I touched a little bit on some of this in Chapter 2, but now I'm going to give you some examples that you can use.

#1: A Powerful Headline

Your headline is the most important part of any ad that you create. You only have ten seconds to catch the attention of the reader. If you don't, expect your ad to be tossed in the garbage.

Ninety percent of your marketing success will come from your headline!

It has been said that an average of five times as many people read the headlines as opposed to reading the copy. That means if your headline doesn't sell then you're wasting 90 percent of your money.

When you're reading the paper or a magazine, what makes you read certain articles? An eye-catching headline that interests you! Well, that's what you need to create when you are sending your customers or new prospects an offer. Grab their attention. You can have the best letter or ad in world, but if you have a crappy headline, forget about it! It won't get read.

When you write your headline think of *who* you're writing it to, who would respond, who wants this. **Your headline isn't for every single person in the world.** Remember, you're going to be going after a specific crowd, not the entire city. This is where I see the most mistakes; everyone thinks their offer is for everyone. It's not!

So what do I want as my headline? Let me explain what you *don't* want; this is what I wasted 90 percent of my marketing dollars on. You don't want your logo, business name, or a picture as your headline! This is what most small business owners do because they copy image advertising that every huge corporate business does.

A good headline will promise your reader a benefit to *them*. It could be a testimonial, it can be controversial, and it *will* state an offer that they can't refuse. You want to grab the attention of your readers and make them say, "I have to read this!"

> All your customers or potential customers care about is...
> **"What's in it for me?"**

The whole purpose of writing headlines that make your cash register ring is to identify the biggest benefits of your operation in your customer's perspective. If you can find ways to benefit the people you are targeting, then you have the recipe for a money tree.

Let me give you some examples of proven headlines that pull huge results for anyone in the bar/restaurant business.

> **Free Dinner**

(No strings attached, no BS, no fine text, not buy one get one free.)

This message would be directed at anyone in your target market

(First name), how would you like to have a beer with the hottest staff in (your town/city)?

You can create a postcard with a photo of your staff on the front and this headline on the back. Buy a mailing list of a certain age group of *single* men and have it sent directly to their mailboxes. Write compelling copy and explain why they need to take advantage of your offer. Tell me what single guy you know wouldn't read the rest of this ad with a headline like this?

Local Entrepreneur Infuriates Local Bar Owners by Giving Away Hundreds of Free Dinners

Exposed!
A Startling Fact about (Your Bar)

How You Can Enjoy a Night Out for Only $xx

Why Women in (city) Choose (your bar) Over Any Other Bar

Warning!
Bar/Restaurant Exposed

This is a great headline you can use for almost anything. All you have to do is explain your story/offer after that.

Tired of how expensive it is to enjoy a night out? Come to ABC Bar and get 50 percent off your tab.

You don't even have to do the entire tab for 50 percent off. Make it up to ten dollars off, but don't say that in your headline; your copy or certificate will say that. (If you are going after new customers, go up to twenty dollars off.)

Discover the hidden secret that all the restaurant/bar owners in (your city) don't want you to know!

This is my favorite because it gets the best response. You can use this with any kind of promo. People love secrets!

Here's a quick, easy way to get a free meal.

People love quick and easy when it comes to solving a nagging problem.

Bar Owner Loses His Mind and Should Be Put in Mental Hospital

ABC Bar Almost Files Bankruptcy Due to Lowest Drink Specials in (City)

Make sure you have a story to tell in your copy that has to do with a crazy offer you are giving away.

Why Everyone in (city) Claims This to Be the Biggest Party of the Year

Does ABC Bar really have the best chicken wings in (city)?

Do you know why ABC Bar is ranked #1 for (whatever you want to put in)?

Using a question in a headline will draw readers to read more if it interests them.

I can go on and on, but I wanted to give you an idea of what I mean by great headlines. The whole idea is to get your reader to keep reading. You want them to say, "What's this all about? I've got to read this."

Remember, before you even write a headline you need to understand *who* your prospect is and what your offer is going to be. Once you know this, you need to think of how you are going to attract that person to keep reading.

If you are trying to get more women in your bar for a martini special or low-carb food menu, the "Why Women" headline is a good way to get women to keep reading. They want to know why other women like them are choosing your bar/restaurant. In their minds they might be thinking they are missing out on something and they need to find out what it is.

Most of the time your headline will be your offer. You want this offer to be irresistible! Let me give you a little advice. If you are trying to bring in new customers and turn them into loyal regulars, give away something for free—ten-dollar gift cards or something worth ten dollars.

Think about it. How much is ten dollars' worth of drinks and food at your cost? Four to five dollars on the high end? Is it worth four dollars to you to bring in a brand-new customer who could possibly turn into a loyal regular?

Are you thinking long-term? You need to!

The one thing that I teach my clients is how to determine the lifetime value of a customer. I'm going to be really brief because I don't want to get off the subject of headlines, but keep it in your head. Let's say you attract a new customer and he starts coming in once a month and spends twenty dollars on average. That's $240 in a year.

Would you give away four dollars for $240? The lifetime value of a customer is far more than $240 in the bar business—but I just wanted to give you a quick example.

It's been proven in the direct marketing industry that the two most powerful headline words are *free* and *you*. Take a look at my favorite headlines I've shown you—what words do you see?

Understand that people these days don't care about you or your restaurant or bar. All they care about is what's in it for them. What do they get? Why should they come to your business? You must give them something! The best part is that when you give them something, you will make more money!

Let me explain a couple more things you should do when using headlines.

1. Don't use all caps, just capitalize the first letter in every word.
2. Attract attention.
3. Set the tone for what you are offering.
4. State your unique selling proposition or a guarantee.
5. Try to stir emotion in your readers, make them want more, get into your readers' heads.

When you start your new marketing plan, test some different ads and see what works best. Once you see what's working, you have yourself a winner.

#2: The Offer

How can you measure marketing response if your potential customer can't take action? You need to create a reason for them to come in and request something or bring in a certificate so you know why they are there. You can offer whatever you want, such as a package deal, 20 percent off their tab, free wings, etc.

You will get the best response with a better offer. Remember, customers are in it for themselves. They get hit with tons of marketing from other business, so all they want to know is what's in it for them. When your potential customers get your marketing piece, you want them to say, "Why wouldn't I do this? I need to take advantage of this!"

So don't be cheap! Your competitors are cheap, I'm assuming, or not, if they are number one in your area. People want deals. They need a reason to choose you over anywhere else. I'm not saying give everything away, but you need to give something away to get new customers in the door. Then it's your job to keep them coming back.

You will also get a better response with compelling copy. Tell customers why you are offering what you are. Tell them about the great atmosphere you have. If you are marketing to men describe the attractive waitstaff. You have to remember that when you are targeting a market, you need to write to the desires of what that market enjoys. You will get a much better response.

Your offer should always be at the top of your marketing, either as the headline or sub headline. Your offer is what is going to drive people into your bar, so make sure it's the first thing they see. Give your potential customers a compelling reason to come to your bar right now. If you have any confidence in your business, you should know that these customers will return and spend more money. This is where you make most of your money: repeat business!

When I'm marketing to people who have never been to my bar, I usually put out an offer that I will break even or make very little money on. I believe I run such a great business that if I can just get new customers in the door, I can keep them coming back, especially when I offer them membership in my loyalty program.

You must be the one, though, to decide what is irresistible for your customers. If you give them a wimpy offer, why should they even come in? You will see that the more you offer, the more they spend and the more new customers will come through your doors.

An offer is not an offer without an expiration date.

You must have an expiration date on every offer; otherwise, people can get this offer anytime, so it's not special to them now. An expiration date creates a sense of urgency—for instance, an "until we run out" special. What the expiration does is tell the customer that if they don't act now, they will miss out. Your main goal in marketing is to sell something *now*, not later.

You must also give a reason for your offer. It doesn't have to be a strong reason just something simple. In celebration of the New Year or your birthday or St. Patrick's day—these are all little reasons, but you must mention why. Half-price burgers—why? Because your kitchen manager made a mistake and double ordered ground beef and you need to sell now! Or you could come up with a cheap draft special for a certain amount of time because you found a case or two of twelve-ounce plastic cups (or whatever size you want) and you are running this draft special to get rid of them.

I send a postcard out to all my customers every single month for $7.50 off their tab because they are a loyalty member. Every month that is their reason to come back in.

At the time I'm writing this I have about 4200 members in my loyalty program. I get about five to six hundred customers back every month using their free $7.50 gift card (which must be used on food), and 88 percent of these customers buy drinks on top of this. Keep them coming back!

#3 A Call to Action

Including a call to action is something that is often missed. Most of your customers are pretty smart people, I'm assuming, but there are some who are not. You must tell them exactly what to do to take advantage of your offer.

If people are confused about your ad they will not respond. Be clear. Do they have to bring in the postcard, do they have to call your bar, do they have to go online and sign up somewhere? If they have to cut out a certificate and bring it in with them before the expiration date, you must explain that in the advertisement.

#4 Compelling Copy

Compelling copy is words that make you want to read more of your ad. Each sentence makes you want to read the next.

Here is an example of a letter that I sent to new movers in my area (yes, you can buy a list of new movers within a certain zip code and get them to come to your bar and turn them into loyal customers).

Local Bar/Restaurant Owner Infuriates His Competition by Giving Away Hundreds of Free Meals in Your Neighborhood

"I'm Buying Your Next Meal Because It's My Way of Welcoming You to the Neighborhood"

Hey Neighbor,

My name is Nick Fosberg, and I own Casey's Pub in Loves Park. I saw that you had just recently moved into the neighborhood, and I wanted to buy dinner. Why? Because I'm that kind of guy. No, this isn't some kind of buy-one-get-one deal. I'm buying you dinner up to $7.50 off, no strings attached!

You see, I do business different from everybody else. Most business owners are trying to get every penny out of you. Don't you agree? I believe that if I can help people and buy them a meal every once in a while, hopefully they will refer their friends and family. When was the last time you were offered anything free without restrictions?

If you're like most people, eating at home is boring. You're at work all day, stressed out by your irritating boss, and the last thing you want to do is take twenty-five to thirty minutes of your time to cook your own meal, or even worse eat another frozen dinner!

Save Yourself the Hassle and Get a Free Dinner Served to You in an Entertaining Establishment with a Friendly Waitstaff

This was just the beginning, but do you see how you capture the reader to keep reading? You want to create a bond with the reader, and you do this by understanding them and their life. You want to relate to them on an emotional level. When you find a way to stir up their emotions and show them you are their solution, you have their trust!

For example, I brought up how eating at home is boring and how they can get away from that and be entertained. Most people go to the bar because they don't want to sit at home; they want entertainment, they want to talk to people who are like them, they want to get their mind off their nagging significant other, they just want to make friends, they want to look at an attractive staff, sometimes they want to feel like they have a family—and they get that from being a regular and knowing everyone at your bar. Not every bar/restaurant has the same customers, but these are several reasons people go to a bar—and there are a lot more.

Think of what your customers want, and tell them how you are their solution. I like to use the formula *problem, agitate, and solve.* I try to determine the problems someone may be facing; then I agitate the situation by identifying how they might be feeling from this problem, and then finally I tell them how my bar—or my offer—is their solution to their problems.

When you write to your customers or potential customers, you need to write like you would talk. Don't write in stiff, formal, elevated language.

Copy is compelling when it communicates that you understand someone 100 percent. You can relate to them and understand their wants and frustrations. Compelling copy is what builds the response of your ads—not the white space, logos, pictures, or name of your bar.

VERY IMPORTANT!
Make sure you use testimonials in your marketing!

You can tell people all day long that you have the best wings, that you have the best staff, that you have the best atmosphere. The only thing they think is that you want their money and that's why you're telling them this. Show them what other people have said.

A testimonial is a statement from one of your customers about your bar. How do you get these? Ask your regulars to give you three to five sentences why they like your bar, how the food is, what the drink specials are like, etc. You want to get positive feedback from them.

Use testimonials in your postcards and sales letters, on your Web site—all your marketing materials. People have seen all kinds of scandals. They are skeptical about what they believe. Using these testimonials from other people like themselves creates credibility. They will believe in you more. When your friend tells you about a great place to eat, most likely you believe him or her and try it out. These testimonials help you create that same effect.

When using a testimonial you want to add the customer's first and last name along with a city and state where they are from. This builds even more credibility. If you don't have a name, prospective clients will probably think you wrote it.

TIP: When you quote somebody in your marketing, use italics type.

If you are friends with local celebrities, such as news anchors or radio personalities, or know someone who is, they are great people to get testimonials from. If you don't know any, send them a letter with a free offer for dinner or wings and one hundred dollars cash to come in. Explain to them you are looking for a testimonial out of the offer to use in your marketing.

Here are some testimonials I use in my postcards and letters.

"Casey's has been a great partner for the RiverHawks over the past five years. Casey's has been a place our fans, players, and staff enjoy going to for the great atmosphere, food, and drink specials. They really know how to treat you right, and I look forward to our continued partnership."—**RiverHawks General Manager Josh Olerud**

"GREAT FOOD…in fifteen years in Rockford, the ONLY bar I've danced on top of is Casey's…so obviously GREAT DRINKS, too!!!"—**Steve Shannon, 97zok**

"Casey's Pub provided the ideal setting, adequate space, and hospitable atmosphere for Brent's Benefit. Thank you, Casey's, for helping our event be a success. We highly recommend your pub for any future occasions."
—The Brent Hubley Family, Loves Park, IL

"Thanks again for a wonderful time. You guys rock! There is no place in town with a better party package like Casey's. Much appreciated."—**Lindsey Graves, Rockford, IL**

"Nick has done great things for families and charity organizations throughout Winnebago County. I would really like to give him credit for helping families pay their medical bills due to unfortunate situations, hosting a charity dinner every month for St. Jude Children's Hospital, and running a fantastic business in our area. There is no other business in our area doing what Nick is doing."
—Mayor Darryl Lindberg, Loves Park, IL

In a nutshell, you want to communicate with your customers or potential customers using compelling copy by creating a personal relationship with them, understanding them, and showing them that **your bar is their solution**. Talk to them with writing as if you were talking to their face.

At first this may be a little hard, but it gets easy. If you need help with writing ads or letters, I provide a service to write them for you, or I can go over what you wrote and make it better.

Add in a testimonial or two to build up some credibility.

#5 The Ultimate Guarantee

Give your clients a guarantee. This adds credibility, and they will feel more comfortable with your offer.

Example: *Come on down to XYZ Bar, and I guarantee you we have the best wings, most attractive staff, and excellent service, or I'll pay for your wings myself!*

This is strong and makes them believe you more—and if someone did come into your bar and said they didn't like your wings, I am sure you wouldn't make them pay for them. Offering a guarantee makes your offer stronger, and you're doing something that you would do anyways if they didn't like the wings.

Make sure you put some type of guarantee in every ad. This will make you stand out over your competition; do you ever see bar ads with a guarantee? Is this guarantee going to "make" or "break" your ad? No! But it can help in someone's decision to come to your bar.

Overview

What you need in every ad is:

1. A powerful headline.
2. An irresistible offer with expiration date.

3. A call to action.
4. Compelling copy that explains why you are their solution.
5. A guarantee.

What you don't need in every ad is:

1. Your logo or pictures that take away from the copy.
2. Blank space.

Remember to understand your customers and create a relationship.

Your customers want to deal with you because they feel they have some sort of relationship with you—because you understand them. **They don't want to deal with a business that just thinks of them as another sale.**

People always expect something at a discount or for free; give that to them and they will feel appreciated. You don't have to do it every time they come in, but they will always remember when you do.

I remember one time I was out of town at a bar, and the manager bought me a drink. I didn't expect that at all. I was shocked and I felt appreciated. I never really knew what that was like until it happened—and that's the same feeling your customers will feel. I guarantee if I go back to that city again, I will definitely be going back to that bar.

An Important Advertising Technique

You don't have to make your ad look like an ad. Sounds crazy, doesn't it? I sometimes try to make mine look like it was written in a newspaper, as an editorial: two or three columns with a great big headline. My marketing course

"Ultimate Direct Marketing for Bar Owners" has several examples you can copy from and use yourself. More information about the course is in the back of the book.

Remember, your goal is to stand out from every other business. Make sure you give them benefits of doing business with you and tell them why you are better than anyone else and why they shouldn't go anywhere else but to your bar.

If you can manage to master the five things you need in every ad, I guarantee you better results. These five easy steps are a great starting point for anyone who is not used to writing direct-marketing ads. It's very simple, and it gets much easier the more you do it. It will actually become fun because you can write about so many different things. You can be funny and weird. People get boring stuff in the mail all the time, so be different and creative.

CHAPTER 6

Your Step-by-Step Guide to Creating Your Own Money Tree (A System for Turning New Customers into Loyal Regulars)

Like I keep saying, your number-one job is marketing and gaining and keeping customers. I will probably say it one hundred more times because if you only get one thing out of this book, this is what I want embedded into your head!

Ninety percent of the success or failure in your business comes from your ability to attract and keep customers and your ability to market yourself to them.

Having a proven marketing system is the number-one secret behind all successful bars. This involves effective systems for developing good relationships with your customers and maximizing the effectiveness of all your ads, postcards, e-mails, and other promotions is the key to your success. Let's take those two franchise chains that serve a ton of wings and beer (don't want to use their names, for all I know I'll get sued!). Anyways these two franchise chains pop up all over the place, and you don't see them going out of business, and they are always busy.

Why? **They have a proven marketing system in place, and they know how to bring in new customers**

and keep them coming back. They understand that this is the most important part of their business.

The advantages of having a system in place are:

1. **There is no limit to your income!** A great sales letter or postcard can bring in thousands of dollars in sales, and once you find one that works, you can produce it as many times as you need to. It's like your printing your own money. Remember what I said before about my first sales letter I sent to businesses? I sent out 240 letters and got over sixteen thousand dollars in sales from it!
2. You will see an improvement in your staff. **They will be very accountable for the success of your new system**, and when your bar is making more money that means they are as well. They feel good about themselves and they feel important.
3. You will control the amount of business you bring in each week. This means you will have the ability to **gain new customers each and every week.**
4. By far the best advantage is that you can put this system on autopilot. Once you find the ads that work for you and the best promotions that work for you, **all you have to do is hire someone to operate this system for you.**

Once you have your marketing system in place, this adds up to the ultimate bar/restaurant business. You will have more freedom and money to do what you want. You can spend more time golfing or boating or whatever it is that you like. **Systems work so that you don't have to spend too much of your time in your business.**

When I first got into the business, I either didn't think about or didn't have the time or skill to create a system. I didn't know how to write successful letters, postcards, news releases, etc. These are all the things you need to be successful—or I should say *really* successful.

A business without a system is inefficient, losing profits, and also losing customers. Do you have a system in place?

There are three ways you can make more profit in the bar business

- Get more new customers every week.
- Increase the value of each customer transaction.
- Get your existing customers to come back more often.

Getting more new customers in your doors, getting your new customers to turn into loyal customers, and getting your existing customers to come back more often is what will increase your profits the most. You can do this for a very low cost and cut out expensive advertising such as radio, TV, and newspaper.

Let me give you some strategies that will explode your business.

Capture your customers' information and generate repeat sales.

This is the most important part of your business. When you have your existing customers' information, you can text them, e-mail them, call them, send them mail, etc. You have every possible way to contact them in a very cost-effective way!

They will only give you their information if they *want* to receive offers from you. This is what you want. They are raising their hands saying, "Send me offers." You don't get that by advertising on TV, radio, newspaper, or other types of advertising.

This allows you to become a welcomed marketer, not a pest, like every other business in your area is most likely looked at. When customers gladly hand over their information to you, they are expecting to hear from you. They want to hear from you. This gives you the ultimate advantage over everyone else in your area.

Do you see how this type of marketing will outperform spending hundreds of dollars in newspaper, TV, and radio ads?

For some reason most bar owners are clueless about how valuable this is. I actually fire employees if they don't capture enough people's information. I'm serious. *That's how important this is.* (Well, they get one chance to improve...If they don't improve or make an effort, I send them on their way or give them slower shifts)

Remember:

It is seven times more profitable to market to your existing customers than to a cold list of people. Who would you rather market to?

It is much easier to get your existing customers to come back to your bar than anyone else. They have been there before, and they like your bar. If they didn't, they wouldn't have given you their information!

What to Ask for

At the very least you need to ask customers for their name, address, cell number, e-mail, and birthday. You can also ask them any other info that you want that you may think may be valuable for you to have, such as what kind of music they like, who their favorite sports teams are in each sport, what bar games they like to play (pool, darts, etc.), and what their favorite menu item is.

When you have information like this in your database, you can then target certain people in your list about a pool tournament or another type of promotion. Make sure you segment your list for men and women.

Why? If you are running a ladies night promotion, you can send only the women a message. This way you are saving hundreds of dollars by marketing to exactly *who* you are trying to attract.

Here's another strategy: on my loyalty list I ask customers if they consider themselves to be an early crowd or late crowd customer. Why would I do this? Because it can save you thousands of dollars over a year! If I'm running a promotion for the younger crowd out from ten to two a.m., I don't want to spend the money to send my offers to the early crowd people. **This is what direct marketing is all about! Targeting exactly who you want or who is most likely to respond.**

If you have a lunch special or daytime promotion, you are better off spending your money on the early crowd people. I'm not saying don't send the daytime offer to your late-night people because everyone eats lunch—unless they are still sleeping from being at your bar the night before! But you will get a much better response from your older early crowd than you will your younger late crowd. You know your customers better than me, so you must use your judgment here.

So How Do I Get Their Information?

It will take a little bit of time to create a big database, but while you are learning everything else about direct response marketing, you will have five hundred people, if not more, in a flash. **This database you create will be the most valuable asset of your business.**

Your customer database is now your primary target market. This will eliminate worrying about paying expensive advertising and losing your ass. This will give you the results you have always wanted and put a chokehold on your competition.

Don't let me confuse you: You should advertise other than to your customer database—this is how you get more *new* loyal customers—but you should spend 80 to 90 percent of your marketing budget on just your existing database. If you invest in my marketing course, you will see multiple ways how marketing to your database will bring in hundreds of *new* customers in addition to your current customers.

I'm sure you've heard of the old fish bowl idea right? People drop in their business card in order to win something, and you grab everyone's information and put it into a database to contact them over a period of time. This is one way to capture names, but there are several others I will go over with you.

Radio, TV, and Newspaper Contests: I know I say don't spend money with high-priced media, but sometimes it is worth it depending on what you are trying to do. One promotion that works really well is to give away a $250 gift card or something valuable where people have to sign up to win.

Tell the advertising sales rep you will give this prize away in exchange for the names of the people who sign up. **If the**

prize is good enough, they won't even charge you for advertising the promotion. The media loves to get high-valued items for free to give away to their audience. You can also tell them to go to your Web site in order to win and fill out a form to capture that info.

Think of it like this. A $250 gift card that might cost you around fifty bucks cost could get you five hundred names or more of people who want to win something from your bar. Creating a database is your number-one goal, and getting these qualified leads for free is a huge advantage for you.

Let me tell you a quick story about Fred, a private client of mine. He called his local radio stations and said that he had one thousand dollars in gift cards to give away and that he would give them to the station, but he wanted to run a contest and collect everyone's information.

The radio station was all over it! We decided to give away ten one-hundred-dollar gift cards so there were more people who could win. We told the radio station that we only wanted to do one one-hundred-dollar gift card per week. So he got ten weeks of radio time, which was about one minute per day Monday through Wednesday (one minute costs seventy-five dollars in his area). *If he had bought this time it would have cost him $2,250!*

To automate everything, I created a simple one-page Web site for him where people would go to enter to win the gift cards. When people signed up at the Web site, all their information was put directly into his database.

Here is a golden nugget: We advertised that no matter what, everyone was a winner. If they went to the site to enter, they would automatically receive a ten-dollar gift card just for signing up. Why would we do this? To get more new customers in the door, obviously. As soon as they signed up to win, they were sent to a "thank you" page telling them to check their e-mail to get their ten-dollar gift card. Once they opened the e-mail the ten-dollar gift card was attached, and all they had to do was print it off and bring it in. Automation is key!

Fred captured the full contact information of 1,364 people, of which 1,127 were brand-new customers that were not in Fred's database! He got 436 people to come in and use his gift cards. After going through all his tabs and calculating the discounts from the gift cards, this brought in an extra $1,354 in sales.

Let's run a quick overview of what Fred did. He gave away roughly $250 in his cost of food and drinks. He got ten weeks of advertising that would have cost him $2,250. He captured 1,127 new people's contact information. He got 436 of them to actually drive into his place and spend money, and he created an extra $1,354 in sales.

Now the real number to look at is the lifetime value of each of these new customers. If he can get one hundred of those people to come back just one time per month and spend twenty-five dollars, that is $2,500 in extra sales per month or thirty thousand dollars per year! **Would you do this for $250?**

Comment Cards: Another way to get your customers' information is comment cards. These are very helpful in many other ways. You learn a lot about what your customers want. You will be able to improve your business and make your customers happy. The reason you are in business is for the customers' needs, not yours. Find out exactly what they want and give it to them!

Do a monthly drawing with the comment cards for a one-hundred-dollar gift card; this is how you get people to participate. At the end of the month, draw a name—or have a certain night you draw and if the person is there to win, they get an extra fifty dollars.

Here is another quick story to show you how important these could be to your business. A private client of mine, Val, created a comment card, and one of the questions was "What are the top three promotions you would like to see us do that we haven't done already or quit doing?"

She had roughly 650 to 700 of these filled out, and after reviewing them she saw that eighty-seven people wanted to see them do a country night. So what did Val do? She gave her customers what they wanted! She picked a slow night that she was trying to pick up, started country night, and doubled her nightly sales within three weeks. It tripled after four.

How could she double or triple her sales so quickly? She had eighty-seven people who raised their hands and said that's what they wanted! She was able to contact them directly, give them an offer to come in during a promotion they wanted, and she also gave them a little bonus gift card if they brought in three or more people with them, as well as letting them reserve tables.

This may sound like a pain in the ass. That is why you hire your staff to get these filled out and go through them. You hire them to put them into a database, and at the end of the week or month you analyze what your customers want. *It's that damn easy!*

Giveaways: Every month you can give away a gift card or any kind of prize you want and have people enter to win. Make sure you're giving away something valuable or you won't get information from as many people as you would like.

Once you put the information in your database, send everyone a postcard for a free meal or something similar. This will drive them back—and remember, put an expiration date on there. Make sure your staff staples the postcard to the receipt so you can see what they spend.

People usually spend more money when they are getting something for free or at a discount.

Vacation packages are a great way to do this as well. There is a company called Vacation Adventures International where you can purchase exotic vacation packages all over the US and also to tropical destinations for as low as fifty to ninety-nine dollars per package depending on the quantity and destinations.

If you're a smaller venue and not able to purchase their minimum of twenty-five packages at a time, they will work with you. I have also set up promotions for different clients in which I give them one of my trips, a marketing plan, and a promotion to increase their sales and build up their database of customers. If this is something you would be interested in, please contact me at www.BarOwnerMarketingSystems.com and leave a message on the contact page.

If you would like more information on the packages you can buy directly from Vacation Adventures, call 1-888-448-3980. Ask for Vito and tell him you got his information from Nick Fosberg. He will give you a courtesy discount as he does with all of my clients.

Partner with Other Businesses (Joint Ventures): This is a *great* strategy. Think of other businesses in your area that share the same type of customers as you. You can create a contest or a giveaway and get *their* customers to sign up to win.

Why would these businesses do this?

1. You are offering something valuable to their customers to win. Why wouldn't any business owner want to give their customers a chance to win something valuable from a noncompeting business?
2. Maybe you can do something for them in exchange at your bar to help them out. Promote their service or

product with signs, or add them to your monthly e-mail for that month with an offer from them.

Some of these business may already have a list of people in their database. Ask them if you can send them some type of free offer. The smart thing to do is to write a sales letter for the business you are going to partner with as if it is coming from them.

For example, say I'm working with an auto repair shop. I would write a letter as if I were the owner of the auto shop. You will get a much better response this way than if you write the letter as if it were coming from you.

Dear Nick,

Hey, it's John from John's Auto Sales. I went out and bought a few gift cards to Casey's Pub in Loves Park to give to my loyal customers. You've been a great customer and I wanted to show my appreciation, so here is a $10 gift card for you!

Why did I pick Casey's? (state what makes your bar better)

If you use this strategy, you should pay for the mailing and do the work since they are giving you access to their list of people.

Businesses I have worked with are tanning salons, pizza restaurants, beauty salons, cell phone stores, auto dealerships, and a few others. Any business that is not a bar/restaurant within a mile or two of you is a possible partner. This is a great way to capture a ton of names. Remember, your goal is to build that list and keep building it.

Another way you can use other businesses is by getting giveaways from them to offer to your customers. This way you are giving them exposure to your customers in exchange for a product or service that they offer.

Another private client of mine lived in an area that was big into snow skiing. He called a resort and told them he wanted to run a promotion where people could sign up to win a weekend trip with lodging and skiing included.

This is what he offered the resort. He told them that everyone who signed up to win would have to leave their full contact information. He said that he would give that full list to the resort to send more offers to, or if they provided some marketing materials to him he would send those offers out in an e-mail to everyone at no charge.

. He got a six-hundred-dollar package that included skiing passes, lodging for two nights, and a free dinner at one of the restaurants. This didn't cost the resort anything, and it got them a ton of exposure. It didn't cost Jason (my client) a penny to give this away. It's a win-win situation for each person involved. It worked out so well they did this for the following three months.

A Simple Goal-setting Task for You

Right now I want you to take out a notepad and write down a goal: how many names you want your employees to get for you by signing up your existing customers. Then jot down five businesses within your area that you could call to see if they would be interested in a joint venture. Be sure to set goals for your employees; tell them they are to get fifty to one hundred names within thirty days. If they do, they all get a bonus. Implement! **Don't procrastinate.**

I would love for you to send me an e-mail or letter, or even give me a phone call, telling me how quickly you built your list to one thousand names and what you did to do it. And if you don't mind, I would like to publish that for other bar owners so they can learn from you as well. You are probably different than most bar owners in that you are motivated to make things happen quickly, but sometimes it takes some success stories to really motivate others to do the same thing.

One of my biggest problems was not being organized and forgetting important things that needed to be done. One of my mentors had me write a list every day of things I needed to do, and then put them in order based on which ones were going to make me the most amount of money. Let me just say that this simple approach, if implemented, can make a big difference in your life.

CHAPTER 7

Staying in Touch with Your Existing Customers

Now that you have all your customers' information, it's time to start marketing to them to get more money in your registers.

Direct Mail

Some bar owners just use e-mail, which is OK, but you won't get the response that you will from direct mail. Yes, e-mail is extremely cheap, but what you want is *results* and more people packing your bar. You won't pack your bar only using e-mail!

Direct mail is highly overlooked in the bar industry and I don't understand why. Actually, I do know why—because bar owners are always approached by sales reps who sell radio, TV, and newspaper advertising. There are not any sales reps selling postcard marketing or writing sales letters for us.

But direct mail is one of the best ways to reach your customers because everyone receives mail, and it's very rare that other bar owners are sending your customers anything by mail! This gives you a huge advantage because you are the only bar reminding them to do business with you.

Make sure you keep mailing to your customers. Sometimes your offer might not be good for someone at that time but it will a month or two down the road. Stay in front of them because people tend to forget about you. Keep telling them why they need to come to your bar over any other bar!

What do you mail to your customers? Postcards, newsletters, and sales letters. Let me explain a little bit about each of these to you.

Postcards: Postcards are very inexpensive. Make sure you send your message out on a brightly colored card. Yellow seems to draw the most attention.

At the very top of your postcard should be the headline. Remember, this is a great offer you are making or an attention-grabbing headline about a promotion you are running. Make sure you have a coupon/certificate on your card so customers have to bring it in to get your offer. Or send them to a Web site or have them call you to get the offer.

As I mentioned before, I use rip cards for monthly mailings to my loyalty customers. Rip cards are just like postcards but at the end of the card is a business card–sized tab that tears off easily. You put your offer on there and all people have to do is tear it right off and put it in their wallet, purse, pocket, or wherever.

I get a much better response with rip cards because some people don't want to take the time to cut out a coupon. Yes, people are really that lazy! Some people don't want to bring in an 8.5 x 5.5 postcard either. So the rip card makes it extremely easy for them.

Rip cards are a little more expensive, about eighty cents apiece depending on how many you mail out, but they are worth it for the better response. Don't forget, all that matters is results. Spend a little more, get better results, which equals higher profits.

Newsletters: Newsletters are a very important way to stay in front of your customers. Customers want to know what's new, and you can let them know about upcoming events, new food specials, new food items, new drink specials, etc.

Staying in the front of your customers' minds with new information is huge. Other bar owners are always trying to take your business, and sometimes your old customers forget about you. Stay in the eyes of your customers every month. This will help with repeat business and referrals.

"But I don't like to write, and I don't know how to create a newsletter."

I thought this would be hard, too, and at first it is a little difficult—but it becomes really easy after writing a few. To start out, write to them as if you were talking to their face. Talk about something that happened to you or tell them something about yourself. Get personal.

Remember, you want to create relationships with these people and make them feel like they really know you. If you just got back from vacation, tell them where you went, what you did, or tell a story about your son or something that happened to you. People love reading stories about other people.

After you get a little personal with your customers, tell them everything that is new with your bar, like upcoming events and promotions. If you are friends with other business owners in your area who are not bar owners, you can put in some offers from these business and charge a small fee, or maybe they can give away some offers for you at their business (joint venture!).

A newsletter really is a fun way to communicate with your customers. You can tell funny stories that happened in your bar, talk about a certain regular everyone knows (just make sure you don't offend them), and put bar jokes in there. I write these so people look forward to reading them. It's rare that people get to read funny and exciting news anymore.

Sales Letters: Bar owners sending sales letters? This is unheard of! Yes, you are right, and you are probably missing out on great opportunities.

I won't get into too much detail because learning how to writing sales letters is a whole other book itself, but let me explain why they can be so profitable for you. Sales letters are a great tool because you can explain everything you want in full detail. You have unlimited amounts of pages you can send.

I have written four-page sales letters to businesses about why they should have their holiday party at my bar. Some people say, "They won't read four pages" If you give them a good enough offer and a great headline, they will read the whole damn thing! Trust me. I didn't think they would either but the marketing coaches I worked with knew way more than I did. So I listened to them and they were right.

Sales letters are not easy to write. I studied copywriting books, manuals, and even hired a professional copywriter to work with me and teach me the techniques I needed to get a great response.

If you are looking for someone to write sales letters for you, I'm now offering this service, so contact my office for more information, or you can leave a message on the contact page at www.BarOwnerMarketingSystems.com.

Text Messaging: This is one of the most common forms of direct-response advertising in the bar and nightclub business. Text messaging is a very powerful marketing strategy because almost everyone has a cell phone, and all cell phones can receive messages (your offer).

I don't know the exact percentage on this, but if I remember correctly from statistics on text message marketing, as high as 98 percent of people read texts they receive. This means that if you send out one thousand texts to your list of people about an offer you have for that day, 980 people are going to read it. Let's say you're giving away a free meal today to everyone who shows this text, and you get a 10 percent response. That's 98 people! Very powerful marketing. Yes, you are giving away ninety-eight dinners but these people are going to drink, or they are going to bring in some people with them who are going to buy a meal plus drinks.

If you are not familiar with text message marketing, there are many businesses online where you can sign up for texting services. I'm working with a service that gives you a thirty-day free trial. Email me at nickfosberg@gmail.com and I can forward your message to them. It's a very easy system to use!

I think one text per week is enough. You don't want to annoy your customers and end up on the opt-out list. If you have several *new* promotions going on in the same week, then send two or three if you have to, but make sure you're not sending the same shit over and over.

How do you track your response? Tell your customers they must show the message to get the offer, and then make sure your staff writes down on check that they used the text message promotion.

On the day you have a promotion, make sure you send out the text four to five hours before the offer will be valid. For example, if you are running a lunch special, make sure customers receive the text message around nine a.m. If you've got a happy hour special, they should get the text message around lunchtime.

E-mail: I send three to four e-mails to my customers per month. Not everyone has e-mail, but it is free for the most part, and some people spend hours on the computer each day and would rather read email than a newsletter sent through the mail.

E-mails don't have to be long. They just include news about an upcoming promotion. You can send out a deal on gift cards and people can pay for them right there. I teach a great way to sell gift cards, and they say that only 80 percent get used!

When you are sending e-mails to customers, make them plain text. Some of online e-mail services offer you templates to choose from, but I don't recommend those. Remember you want to create a personal message; **you want your customers thinking you are talking directly to them.** If you send something out fancy they will think you sent it out to everyone (which you did). But when you send an e-mail to a friend it's plain, right? This is exactly what you want.

If you choose to e-mail a newsletter, you might want to have images and use a template because everyone knows newsletters get sent to your whole list. But if you are sending out an offer to get someone to come in, write it as if you only sent it to them. You will get a much better response.

Collecting E-mails Digitally

In today's world, technology is changing by the second. What was new yesterday could be old a week from now. The Internet is now available in the palm of your hand. So if you plan on being in the bar business much longer, you need to have a Web site and you need to use Facebook for one very important reason: collecting people's information.

At the top of the screen, your Web site must have a opt-in box with a great headline offering something for free in order. This will get your potential costumer to sign in or "opt in."

People get asked for their e-mails all the time, and then they get spam "junk mail" and it's annoying to them. So for you to get them to opt in, you need to offer something valuable and worthwhile to them.

If you go to the Web site for my bar, www.CaseysPub.net, you will see right when you hit the page I'm offering a free gift card every month. I get people signing up all the time for this and it's a great way to get them in the door to buy drinks.

Your Web site only has two jobs:

1. Giving people information about your bar and telling them why you are better than any other bar in the area.
2. Capturing their information so you can market to them every month.

Collecting E-mails from Facebook

Since the creation of Facebook Pages, you can now offer your customers the same thing that is on your Web site opt-in and collect their information.

You can hire someone to create what is called a "squeeze page," which is like a your own Web page on Facebook. The squeeze should, as always, give your customers an offer in exchange for their information.

To see an example, Google "Casey's Pub Loves Park, IL" or go on Facebook and search "Casey's Pub Loves

Park." Make sure you check out the "Pages" page. We do have a friends page still up, which is what everyone had before the "Pages" page came out. You will notice that if you click the Like button you can get a free offer, and once you click it a form pops up to get your information.

Everyone is on Facebook so I encourage you to add this to your marketing strategy. If you need help, please contact my office and we can do this for you.

CHAPTER 8

Checking Your Aim

I'm going to keep this chapter short, and a lot of it is going to be repeat information, but it's time to check in on a very important point: hitting your target audience effectively.

You must test every ad that you do. Any time you are spending money to get people in your doors, you need to test it out first. I don't want you to send ten thousand letters to a large list of people. Start small with just one hundred or three hundred and see what kind of response you get. If you get a great response, send out another thousand or more and see how that goes.

Obviously if your mailing doesn't get a good response, you know you need to change something or give a better offer. If you have a successful ad, maybe you can make it better, so change the headline and see if you get better results. You should always find ways to improve your response.

How Do You Track Your Marketing?

We've gone over a lot of ways to track your marketing, so I want to refresh your memory and give you an all-inclusive resource for tracking.

The best ways to track your results is coupons or certificates. When people bring these in, you will know where they came from and from which ad. You will know which ads are working and which are not.

You can also use a Web site to track your ads. Tell people to go to a certain Web site to print something off or sign up for a free offer. Again, if you need help with this service you can contact my office. We can usually get you a site like www.Caseyspub.net for five to seven hundred dollars. It has opt-in form to capture e-mails and a place for people to subscribe to Facebook and Twitter. Most companies will charge over a thousand dollars for this.

You can have people call your bar to get the discount. Have your employees take down their information and send them a gift card or whatever you are offering in the mail, or they can come pick it up. This method has worked great for me. Remember the $16,091 sales letter I told you about? Customers had to call me in order to set up their party. I knew how many I booked because they had to call. I then tracked the sales for each party to see how much money I made from the entire mailing.

You can also tell people to "mention this ad" in order to get a discount. I'm sure you've seen this before. It is used in almost every industry.

So as you can see, there are many ways to track your marketing, but the easiest way is to have customers bring in a coupon or gift card. Remember, you must have your employees staple the coupon to the check and keep these. At the end of the expiration date, add up the totals and the discounts and see what your profits are! It's that easy. If you lost money, you need to change the ad or go after a different group of people with that offer. If you lost money with an ad, don't run the same ad! Or at least don't run it in the same place.

You can't do this with traditional advertising! Anything that is measured can be improved.

Make sure you:

1. Have a tracking device on every ad. You must decide what you want to track, new customers brought in, total sales, and profits.
2. Put a form together to track your results. Make sure all your employees know how to handle these coupons, and let them know how important it is that you track and monitor this.
3. Hold yourself and your employees accountable by following up with all your employees. Make sure they know that you are reviewing all the results.
4. Keep a record of this data in a spreadsheet or just write it down on paper.
5. Always think of how you can improve your results. Ask employees or customers for their input. (It is also a good idea to show sales letters and postcards to your customers and get their opinion as well.)

Once you get all the tracking down, this will be the most exciting part of the business. This is where you see the profits. You will see positive numbers, and then you can produce more and more. It's like printing your own money.

It does require discipline and patience. You can only test a few things at a time. If you are lazy and don't care, then testing isn't for you, but if you want to know whether or not you're spending your money on the right marketing, then I suggest you take a little time to get this down.

CHAPTER 9

Double Your Regulars, Double Your Profits, Double Your Vacation Time

The number one way to capture highly qualified information and repeat sales is to create a loyalty program. If you have one, great! You are one step ahead—but are you using it the most profitable way?

The reason you must have a loyalty program is because they bring customers back more often to spend more money. I bet you even have a loyalty card in your wallet—a gas card, a credit card that gets points, a rewards card. I remember when I had to go buy a new iPod that I went to a certain store because I could rack up points and get a free gift card. When I remodeled my house, I only went to a certain hardware store to get the points on my card, and I ended up receiving $750 back because of all the purchases.

This is the same exact system you need for your bar.

Every bar needs a loyalty program to get its customers to come back more often and to **turn new customers into loyal regulars.**

If you have a POS system then you probably already have some type of loyalty program in there. If you don't have a POS system, you can still create a loyalty program, but the way it's set up will be a little different.

Let me give you some tips on how to create a bulletproof loyalty system.

What Are You Going to Offer?

A loyalty program must have incentives; otherwise, why else would anyone join? As always, **the better the incentive the more people you are going to get to sign up for your program.** Here are a few things to consider:

- $X amount in free gift cards each month.
- $ amount of free lunches or dinners each month.
- Free T-shirt for joining.
- Free birthday meal.
- X percentage off on the tab on certain days.
- X percentage off food every time they come in.
- Free drink every time they come in (if legal in your state).

You can partner with another business and give them offers from them as well. **The more valuable you make it the more people you will get into it.**

How Are You Going to Deliver the Offer?

There are several ways you can deliver these offers to loyalty members.

☑ Direct Mail
☑ Text message
☑ E-mail

☑ They bring in a loyalty card to receive offer

Yes, e-mail is free and text messaging is only two to four cents a message, but if you want the best response, you need to send customers something in the mail every month. Direct mail is very, very, very reliable and is the most powerful marketing strategy there is. As I said before, I send a rip card every month. I suggest you do the same thing.

Free Program or Charge Them?

Some businesses charge customers anywhere from one dollar to twenty each month to join their loyalty program, depending on what they are giving away. You can create any kind of program you want. You can have multiple programs for your various customers. That's completely up to you. There is no right or wrong way to do it, as long as your customers are getting a higher perceived value than what you are charging.

Make sure you have a free package, though! You don't want to miss out on capturing a single person's information.

For example, if you did charge a fee it would be something like five dollars a month but customers get twenty dollars a month in gift cards. Send them an envelope with four five-dollar gift cards that can only be used one time per visit. This gets them to come back more often. Or if your average meals are eight dollars, you can give them four free meals, which is thirty-two dollars. Charge ten dollars a month, and they get twenty-two dollars in saving each month.

You might be thinking that you're going to lose your ass, right? Wrong. People are going to drink, people are going to bring someone with them, and this is going to bring people back more often. What if you get a customer who only comes in once a month to sign up for this? Now he or she is obligated to come back four times per month.

What Do You Need to Get Started?

- You need a sign-up sheet. You can even buy an iPad and sign people up that way so you don't have to input their information later.
- You need some type of card that customers bring in to show they are loyalty members. You can also get the little key chain cards.
- You need a way to import members' information into a database. If you have a POS system with a loyalty program in it, then you can use that. Otherwise, most people use excel through Microsoft.
- You should create a thank-you letter to send to members after they join. This letter should also have a gift card with an expiration date attached to bring them back in within two weeks of sending it out.
- You need a way to stay organized with all this. (This is the hardest part, but once you get it down it's worth it…or you can have all this taken care of for you! I'll tell you more about that in a minute.)

How Do You Get Your Staff on Track?

Hold a meeting with your staff about your new program to make sure they all understand it. It's very important they understand what is going on because they are going to be the ones signing people up.

To get the best results, you need to have a contest with your staff. I give away fifty dollars cash to the person who signs up the most people each month. This creates competition between the staff. I also tell them they will get more hours, which really helps as well.

When I work with my clients, I teach them that their bartenders and servers are not just bartenders and servers. They are salesmen and women. **They need to sell customers on why this is a good deal.**

You need to put signs all around your bar. It will be your job or the bar manager's job to stay on top of your staff about asking customers to join. I sat down with my staff and told them that after they serve customers their first drink, they are to tell them about the loyalty program or give them the loyalty sheet to read over. This is their job, and if they don't do it they are fired.

When they approach customers, your staff can even tell them that the bar running a contest and whoever signs up the most customers wins cash and gets more hours. People will sign up just to help their server or bartender out. Wouldn't you feel bad if someone asked you to join to help them out and you said no? Especially if it's free and you're getting a good value out of it.

I want to emphasize why building this is mandatory. It's not hard to get two to three thousand names in six to eight months. If you have a slow night and want to pick up business, you can hit two thousand of your loyal customers on their phones and e-mail instantly. Send out a 2-percent-off-tab text, or whatever. Even if you only get ten or twenty customers from that text, it's way better than what you would have had.

What Do You Do When You Have People Signing Up?

When you first start this program, be ready to have someone put all this info into a spreadsheet. Make sure that all your sign up sheets are organized in one spot. Dedicate this job to a staff member. You don't need to worry about taking the time to enter in all this information. **You most important job is marketing and making sure your employees are staying on top of getting loyalty members.**

CHAPTER 10

30 Days to Getting Your Number-one Asset Up and Running

Your #1 Asset: Your Loyalty Program

WEEK 1

Within your first week, all this should be complete (the loyalty cards may take time for delivery).

1. Think of what you are going to offer, what your customers going to get when they sign up.
2. Get one thousand loyalty sign-up sheets printed.
3. If you have a POS system with a built-in loyalty program, order one thousand loyalty cards. Make sure they will work with your system. The cards will need to be numbered and in sequence. Talk to your computer POS company about what you need. If you don't have a POS system just order the cards; they don't have to be numbered or in sequence. (You need something for customers to bring in to show that they are members regardless.)
4. Have a meeting with your staff and tell them about your program. Explain to them that this is

mandatory and if you catch them not asking people after they get their first drink they will lose hours. The second time they lose their job. It is very important to show them you are serious and that there will be consequences. Remember, this is the number-one asset you will have. How soon do you want it?

5. Have a spreadsheet made up ready to add all these names. The first three months there will be a ton of loyalty members signing up. You should have at least one thousand members in two to three months. Make sure your spreadsheet has a category for every question you want to ask your customers, or ways that you can identify what kind of person they are.
6. Get table tents and banners from your beer vendors made up about your new program.
7. Start tracking every day who is doing the best job. Put up the results each week so employees know their numbers. This creates competition! That's what you want.

WEEKS 2–3

Press release: Now that you have your loyalty program in place and are capturing names, send out a press release to local media (newspaper, TV, radio stations) about your new loyalty program. This is a way to reach thousands of people for the price of a piece of paper.

Here is the definition of a press release in case you don't know what one is:

> *A press release, news release, media release, press statement or video release is a written or recorded communication directed at members of the news media for the purpose of announcing something*

ostensibly newsworthy. Typically, they are mailed, faxed, or e-mailed to assignment editors at newspapers, magazines, radio stations, television stations, and/or television networks. Commercial press release distribution services are also used.

The use of press releases is common in the field of public relations (PR). Typically, the aim is to attract favorable media attention to the PR professional's client and/or provide publicity for products or events marketed by those clients. A press release provides reporters with an information subsidy containing the basics needed to develop a news story. Press releases can announce a range of news items, such as scheduled events, personal promotions, awards, new products and services, sales and other financial data, accomplishments, etc. They are often used in generating a feature story or are sent for the purpose of announcing news conferences, upcoming events or a change in corporation.

There are multiple places online to learn how to write a press release, or if you would like me to write a release for you, you can contact my office.

Press releases are great because you can get hundreds, even thousands of dollars' worth of free publicity from one single piece of paper. Even if you pay someone to do it you will still come out ahead if your release is newsworthy.

The very first time I sent out a press release was when I created the charity promo where I help pay for people's medical bills. I had a huge, two-page write up with a full-color picture in my paper that is distributed to over 175,000 people. I was interviewed on TV two different times. I was on the radio talking live about it. **If I were to have paid for all this exposure, it would have been well over ten thousand dollars.**

Online sign-up: You need to set up a way for people to join your loyalty program online. If you have a Web site, great! If not, you better get with the real world! Everyone has the Internet on their phone these days, and everyone is using computers to get information about local bars and restaurants. Times are changing, and so are the ways our customers get and look for information.

Have your Web designer create a place on your Web site to sign people up for your loyalty program. Make sure you ask for all the information that is on your loyalty sheet that people fill out in your bar. Make sure that when this form is filled out online, an e-mail goes to you or your manager so you know to add the person to your main database.

Many bars and restaurants have Web sites that are not designed to capture information or tell their customers why they are better than everyone else. If you would like to set up a consultation to go over your site or have one built, I would be more than happy to help you with this.

Anytime you are using a Web site to capture information from a customer, make sure your opt-in box (where they input their information) is in the top right-hand corner of the page. You want to make it easy for them to find it. Go to www.Caseyspub.net to get an example of what my page looks like.

Facebook: Now that you have your Web site up and going with your loyalty program, you need to get on Facebook and type in this message as one of your posts: *Click this link to get (whatever you are offering in your loyalty program $x amount a month in free gift cards or whatever).*

When you type in this message, click the link button and input the Web address for your sign-up sheet on your Web site. This way when people click the link, it takes them directly to your site with the sign-up form and they don't have to search for it on your Web site. **This is one of the fastest free ways to get people into your program.**

Tip: Have a staff member keep posting this four to five times per day, hour by hour. So many people use Facebook on their phones and check updates, so each time you post this message you will be at the top with most recent posts. You should do this for four to six weeks straight and then do it one or two times per week after that.

Week 4

Joint ventures: This is the same concept as in promoting your bar through an offer. Ask businesses in a different industry but with similar customers to promote your loyalty program through their mailing list in exchange for money—or better yet give them a one-hundred-dollar gift card to your bar. You can send out a sales letter or postcard to their customers or have flyers made up to leave on the counter for customers to pick up.

You can also get in contact with local business owners who have a lot of employees and see if they would hand fliers out to them. If you are offering some type of discount on food, this could be very beneficial to their employees during lunchtime or dinner after work.

Referrals: Start asking your regulars if there is anyone they know who would want to take advantage of your loyalty program. Give them some type of incentive for signing people up, a ten-dollar gift card for every ten people they sign up, for example. This only costs you two to three dollars and it's worth it! Trust me, the more names and contact information you have, the better you are.

Have your staff members get on the phone and call friends and family to sign them up. Give them an incentive as well! The more you give, the more you will receive. Paying for the leads is worth it in the long run because you will be able to contact a very targeted audience extremely cheaply.

Why My Approach Will Skyrocket Your Business with Very Little Effort or Change to Your Business

No matter what, direct marketing is your answer to increasing your income and giving you the lifestyle you have always wanted. This book has given you everything you need in order to start using direct marketing in the most powerful and profitable ways.

Quit wasting money on expensive mass media avenues. **You need a targeted approach to hit exactly who you want: paying customers who are just like your regulars.**

There is no marketing strategy that is more powerful then direct marketing. Remember, you are able to test every ad or strategy that you do for very little investment.

Not everything you try is going to work, but you need to test as much as possible. Like I said, start with three to five hundred targeted. If you get a great response or even break even, then keep doing it to more people.

Your main goal no matter what is to capture the information of every single person who walks in your doors. Once you start building your list it, gets bigger and bigger every day. Within two to three months you are going to have the capability to target one to three thousand people—100 percent of whom *want to hear from you. This is powerful shit!*

You have become the welcomed marketer, and this is going to give you the ultimate advantage over your competition and give your customers a reason to choose you over them.

By now I'm sure you agree with me 100 percent on this approach. It's common sense, right? You can't go wrong with this…but you may be thinking, *This sounds like a lot of work* or *I'd rather just have this done for me.* **This next chapter is for the bar owners who want to put another one to two thousand dollars cash in their pockets week after week without having to create Web sites, ads, loyalty programs, or anything else I mentioned.**

CHAPTER 11

How to Put Another $1,000–$2,000 in Cash Right into Your Pocket Week After Week by Not Doing a Damn Thing but Watch Your Register Ring

There are four reasons bar/restaurant owners are not happy with the amount of work they put into their bar or the profit they bring in each month.

1. They **do not** communicate with their lost customers.
2. They **do not** communicate with their existing customers.
3. They **do not** have a **proven** system for capturing customer information.
4. They do not properly segment their customer list.

You might be thinking, "Well my regulars are in here three to four times every week and they have been for the last three to four years." Sure, you really don't have to market to these people, but you should. They will appreciate what you do for them. Give back to the ones who make you successful!

What I'm really talking about, however, is the majority of your customers who only come in once a week or three times a month. Having this system in place will get them back more and more, and you will see more money in your pocket than you ever have.

When I first created my customer database I realized:

- I had to have one, no matter what!
- It was a headache to manage but it was worth it.
- It was a challenge managing all the mailings, e-mails, and texts…but eventually I figured out how to systematize it (not a fun process).

This is another reason I started Bar Owner Marketing Systems. I realized how vital a loyalty program was, and I realized how difficult it was to manage. You and everyone else probably don't want to take the time to learn how to organize and structure this system. **Wouldn't you just like to have it all done for you? Wouldn't it make your life ten times easier if you didn't have to worry about marketing again?**

My Mastermind Coaching and Done-for-You Programs: Your Simple Solution to Fast Profits without Any Work—and It's 100 Percent Risk-free for Sixty Days

Have any of your sales reps said, "Spend x amount of dollars on ads with me this month, and if you are not happy with the results then you don't pay us"? I didn't think so. Well, this is what I offer my private coaching clients.

I guarantee 100 percent of my services and products. If you are not happy with the results, then I don't deserve to keep a penny of your money. Now if your advertising sales reps would do this for you…they would be out of business because their marketing doesn't work and you will never be happy with it. Am I right?

So I have two offers, and they both are risk-free to you. If you are not happy with the results I bring you, YOU DON'T PAY! No fine lines, no BS. I offer the most brass balls guarantee in the bar business because I know my marketing works and I have *multiple* bar owners around the country to agree with me.

"I feel very fortunate that I responded to Nick's e-mail and thus began a business relationship that I believe will last for many years. Nick's immediate 'get down to work' approach wasted no time in generating sales and profits for my businesses.

"I was impressed with the investment Nick makes in his own continuing education, spending thousands of dollars on coaches and teachers to expand his knowledge of the marketing and promotions businesses, and I am delighted to tap into his expertise to help me. ***He is continually improving himself for the sake of his clients.***

"It was also reassuring to me that Nick has turned around a struggling business himself and made it very profitable. Unlike so many consultants, ***Nick is actually working in the trenches on a daily basis and truly experiences the same challenges that I do and thus can give me specific solutions to my challenges.***

"Sometimes the little things we do in life have enormous impact, By taking ten minutes to make one phone call to Nick, I began a relationship that will not only put tens of thousands of dollars in my bank account but gave me a new way to look at my business and great new ideas to help me expand my thinking. ***I've been in the bar/restaurant business thirty-five years****, and this young man knows how to increase sales better than anyone else I know."***—Tom Beckmann, West Allis, WI, owner of Magoo's Sports Pub, Painted Parrot (Caribbean restaurant)**

"Working with Nick has been fantastic! In ***less than eight weeks*** *we have acquired over three hundred loyalty rewards members and we've* ***booked thirteen parties!*** *Our virtually nonexistent Friday and Saturday nights have become* ***pleasantly steady, and I know we'll continue to grow.*** *Nick is great at working with my hectic schedule and helping me apply his strategies to our bar to make them as effective as possible.* ***With the results I've seen so far,*** *I can't wait to see what happens as we take the next steps!*
—Clair, Players Lounge, Plover, WI

"Within the first two months of working with Nick and using his marketing system, ***I booked seventeen parties from using his sales letters.*** *With Nick creating a loyalty program for my bar, it has really brought in* ***more*** *business and keeps* ***new*** *customers coming back more often.*

*"I would recommend Nick to any bar owner who is looking to increase their sales and decrease their marketing expenses."***—Diane Bee, owner of Wilson Night Club, Wilson, WI**

Your First Option...If You Want To Do Everything On Your Own

You can invest in my course ***"The Ultimate Direct Marketing Course for Bar Restaurant Owners,"*** which is filled with most of the content that is in this book plus more low-cost techniques and strategies. But the real value in this course is that it provides you with all the proven ads, letters, postcards, etc., that I personally use, as well as my coaching clients. These come on a CD-ROM, and all you have to do is input your information. It's really that easy.

This is similar to a toolbox of ready-to-use tools to flood your doors with customers.

I guarantee this course with a twelve-month, ten-thousand-dollars-money-in-your-pocket guarantee. If you don't put an extra ten thousand dollars in your pocket, all of which will come from what you use in this course, **then I will refund your money, no questions asked.**

Your Second Option... If You Want Everything Done For You

You can apply for my Mastermind Coaching and Done-for-You Programs.

This option is very limited and is only for serious and motivated bar owners. I only work with a select handful of private clients each month, and during the summer it's even more limited. I'm from the Midwest, and when we get sunny weather, I cut my working hours down to five hours per week, and the rest of the time is for the boat and my family. So if there isn't room, I can put you on a waiting list.

One of the most valuable components of my coaching programs is that I only work with one bar owner per twenty-mile radius. **This is an area-exclusive opportunity!** I do this because I can't guarantee my services if I'm helping your competition. **The purpose of these programs is to set you aside from everyone else in your area and give you the unique advantage over everyone else.**

I take care of 95 percent of your marketing and create the **most effective and low-cost** marketing system that is going to bring you boatloads of new customers, **double** your profits, and double your loyal regulars the in the shortest amount of time.

With each of my coaching and done-for-you marketing programs, I offer a sixty-day risk-free test drive. This is how this works. I will get some general information from you about your bar. I will tell you exactly what I can do for you and the results you will get.. If you like what I say, then I put my automated systems to work for you. If you do not get the results I say you should expect after sixty days, I will refund 100 percent of your money, no questions asked.

I'm not sure what options you may be looking for, but this is just a brief overview. The next few sections will give you 100 percent of the details about my marketing course that you can do on your own, as well as my coaching programs where I bring in boatloads of new customers and sales for you.

Here is just a short list of what I can do for you:

- **Double** your regulars even on a shoestring budget.
- Book ten to fifteen parties of thirty to sixty or more at your bar, month after month. (These parties will bring in five hundred dollars minimum each time. That's five thousand dollars minimum each month, **sixty thousand minimum per year.**)
- Get **new** movers in your area to come to your bar before your competition gets to them first. (How would you like to be able to get people who just moved into your area and get them turned into your regulars before they do?)
- Handle 95 percent of your marketing for you so can enjoy **more** time off and a **steady stream of profit filling your safe.**
- Create **profitable lo-cost promotions** for you month after month that will keep your bar going with fresh, new ideas to keep customers from being bored with old promos.

- ☐ **Plus much, much more…**

Cavett Robert, the founder of the National Speakers Association, said, **"Experience is not the best teacher because the tuition is too high. Learn from other people's experience!"**

This statement is very true. I've spent thousands of dollars in tuition and also learned from other people's experience. If you are looking for the easy way out and want everything to be handed to you without having to go through all the trial and error I did, then you need to read the next two sections.

If you would like to get a free twenty-minute marketing consultation with me to see what your best options are, or if you want more information about my products and services go to this Web site and fill out the contact form:

www.BarOwnerMarketingSystems.com

Or call **1-815-669-0780**

Whichever you do, leave a message that you have read my book and would like the free consultation. I don't offer this to anyone else—only to bar/restaurant owners who have invested in my book or other products.

Bonus Section 1

The Ultimate Direct Marketing Course for Bar Restaurant Owners

I'd like to introduce the only bulletproof system for bar owners looking to get ahead and dominate their competition. This course will teach you how to thrive, prosper, and profit right now with the time-tested, proven, yet cutting-edge and radically different system for attracting new, loyal customers. It literally changes everything! This system is guaranteed to put an extra ten thousand dollars in your pocket, and if it doesn't, you don't pay a dime for it.

Are you ready? Because this is like nothing you've ever seen, read, or possessed before!

If you are a bar owner and you've been doing well in recent years despite being an advertising victim, constantly wasting money, not really knowing what works and what doesn't, and reinventing the wheel too often, you're probably getting where you're going by paddling faster and harder—without a failsafe navigation system. I'm here to **warn you**: those "generous days" are over and gone forever. If you are marketing like every other bar owner in your area, you are not going to get the results you want, and if you are number one in your area, I will guarantee you can you can increase your sales by 15 to 30 percent while slashing your marketing costs in half.

The truth is, most bar owners are using wasteful "mass advertising" techniques, and it will soon catch up to them if it hasn't already. There are many bar owners who can't even afford to spend one hundred dollars because they are scared of getting the same results they have been getting—nothing, or very little to the point that they are not even breaking even on their marketing. How do they expect to make it? Half-price drinks? That's too much work for too little money, if you ask me.

Bar owners need to know how to *systematically*, efficiently, affordably target OUR ideal, money-in-their-pockets, high-value customers. If you are willing to be honest and admit you don't really have a reliable marketing system, then you are going to count this chapter as a life-altering event.

Can You Relate to This?

If you are a bar owner who uses expensive advertising methods such as TV, radio, and newspaper advertising, you know that the money you spend is not getting you the real results you want. You might break even and maybe make a small profit, but do you even know who is coming in because of your ads? Do you track who comes in from which methods you are using? This may seem hard to do, but in reality it is very easy when you use what I'm about to share with you.

What you need is a marketing system that delivers a *powerful message* or offer to *only people who want to hear from you.* A system that only attracts the people you want to deal with, such as your regulars. Is this even possible? *Yes.* And it is now more vital than ever. Making a top income through sheer persistence and patience while using "mass advertising" just isn't possible in a tougher economy. And in the new, emerging economy, it'll be the wrong skill set altogether.

If you can be open-minded to a radically different approach that makes a life in the bar business infinitely more pleasant and increases income exponentially with less stress and struggle—then I can totally change your income and day-to-day experience virtually overnight, just as I have for other bar owners around the country.

My $10,000 Money-in-Your-Pocket Guarantee

Written Guarantee #1: 100 percent, no-risk, no-hassle, no-B.S., twelve-month, money back guarantee.

If at any time within one year you aren't completely thrilled, head over heels happy with my systems, you can send them back and get a full refund. This guarantee is very straightforward. You don't need a note from your mother. There isn't any teeny, tiny fine print. If you aren't happy, return it and get an immediate, full refund. Period.

Take twelve months to look it over. Read the manuals. Listen to the CDs. Use the system in your business. Discover how the system can generate good, loyal customers every day. Use the whole system. Put it to work for you. Generate new customers, more referrals, higher average checks. Benefit from it. Make money with it. And then, if you aren't totally elated with the system or the results for any reason, I insist you send it back for a prompt and cheerful refund. I'll buy it back from you, unconditionally!

Written Guarantee #2: $10,000 in-your-pocket, one-year guarantee!

I'm so sure the system will work for you that I am willing to make you an unheard of guarantee: You will put **at least ten thousand dollars in additional income** in the bank in the next twelve months. Every penny of this money will be directly attributable to my system.

This is money that you would not have otherwise had. It'll come directly from customers that came from the system. If you keep and use your system past the first ninety days and you can show me proof that you have implemented at least one of my strategies, if at the end of a full year you write me a letter and can honestly say you didn't put at least ten thousand dollars in the bank that you wouldn't have otherwise, I will still refund every penny you paid. You are the sole judge and jury. If you try my system and it doesn't make you money, send it back for a full refund.

This means that you can get, review, and use my system without risking a single penny of your money. **Zero risk.**

Ask yourself this question: Would I make a guarantee like that and sign my name to it if I didn't think the system would far exceed your expectations? I know this system will work for you—no matter what level your business is at right now. That's why I offer you such a rock-solid guarantee.

The Ultimate Direct Marketing System for Bar Owners will show you:

- How to build a loyalty program for your bar that will be the most valuable asset you will ever own and give you ultimate advantage over your competition.

- How this loyalty program will keep your existing customers coming back **more often to spend more money.**
- How to target new movers in your area and get them to become regulars at your bar **before they even visit your competition.**
- How to determine **who** your best customer is, **how** to find more them, and how to get them into your bar in the most **cost-effective way.**
- How to build relationships with your existing customers through your marketing and make them feel like they are **"family"** at your bar. (Business is all about relationships, no matter what industry.)
- How to get the local media to call you and **promote your bar at no cost.**
- How to cut your marketing costs in half so you can put more money in your pocket.
- How to get expensive newspaper, TV, and radio advertising for **free.**
- What you must have in every ad to make your customers respond quickly so you get money in your pocket **now** and not later.
- HOW TO **DOMINATE** YOUR COMPETITION EVEN WITH **HIGHER PRICES.**

That's only a small sample of what you will discover!

Any one of these could add thousands of dollars to your yearly income. All of them could possibly double your sales.

I broke my proven system into a simple, step-by-step guide. I made this so easy you could literally hand it to your manager and have him or her take over from here on out. Let's quickly go over what is included in this system.

Moneymaking Component #1: No Brainer, Fast Implementation! (a $3,000 value)

I've included all my proven ads, postcards, sales letters, strategies, etc. I've done all the hard work so you don't have to spend thousands of dollars on other marketing courses, going to seminars, or hiring other experts to tell you what to do.

All this profit-boosting information will be on a CD and in a manual. All you have to do is put your information in and get your marketing piece delivered. Yes, it's really that **E-A-S-Y!**

Can you imagine having a manual of proven ads and marketing secrets to pick from that will literally put thousands of extra dollars in your bank account? **There is nothing else like this currently available to bar owners.**

Moneymaking Component #2: Quick Start Guide (& CD) to Quick Profits (a $1,500 value)

This guide is going to be your **groundbreaking marketing lifesaver.** I made it so simple and easy to understand how direct marketing works and how to use it that you could be out of state and still run your business more effectively. I go over the five rules you **must** follow in every ad and the three must-have crucial components to direct-response marketing.

This manual is going to give you step-by-step instructions on how to build the most valuable asset you will ever own. This asset will be how you are going to communicate with your existing customers and put an "iron cage" around them to protect them from your competition.

This "secret" asset combined with my proven letters and ads is going to create a **relationship** with your customers! Business is all about relationships, and once you create a relationship through your marketing with your customers, you will have created an absolute gold mine!

Money-making Component #3: Hands-on Personal Assistance (a $1,000 consultation value)

I'm going to give you two **free** critique certificates that you can use for me to review any ad, letter, or postcard you decide to create yourself. I will personally look over it and tell you how to make it better, what's missing, and if it has the right message going to the right market.

I'm also going to give you a **free 30-minute consultation** by phone to ask me any questions you may have to get you off to a quick start. Coaching is what made me so successful because I had a mentor to help me when I was stuck, and I want to make sure that doesn't happen to you.

I'm still in coaching programs today. I spend $1,400 a month with three different mentors and organizations for help and support. Marketing is always changing, and I pick up priceless new marketing strategies and techniques every month.

Why do pro athletes have coaches? Why does the president have advisors? Because no matter who you are, you still need guidance at times. **Two heads are better than one**. Don't you agree?

This is the only 100-percent proven, reliable, and profitably marketing system for bar owners. It is **everything** you need for a true marketing *system*. That means you go to bed at night—every night—*knowing* (not wondering, wishing, praying, hoping) where your sales will be, even during slow traditional times. This is a system in sync with the emerging new economy, where customers have more confusing and competing choices than ever, traditional "mass adverting" readership is drastically falling, people are overwhelmed with communication and technology, and the way people used to shop or look for things to do has changed.

You can't afford to get stuck in the "old" days. This is a system with direct, targeted outreach to carefully selected, money-in-their-pocket customers—literally the opposite of costly, wasteful mass advertising and marketing. Every marketing technique and strategy that doubled my sales within an eight-month span is all compressed in this one system, and now it is yours to try, play with, examine, **totally risk-free for one year!**

That's $850 in bonuses just for you if you act within the next forty-eight hours on this risk-free opportunity that can transform your business.

Now, there are a lot of extra goodies and surprises that I have for you if you decide to take action and make a smart investment for your business—because I believe in over-delivering, and when you work with me you always get more than you paid for and more than you expected.

Bonus #1: One month free of my Silver Coaching membership and Done-for-You marketing services (a $350 value)

This is a huge bonus! I'm going to give you one month **free** of my Silver Coaching Program. The monthly investment is $350 per month for this program, but I'm giving you one month absolutely free. This includes **one private twenty-minutes phone consultation each month** to go over any questions you may have about marketing, promotions, building your lists, increasing your profits, etc.

If at the end of one month you feel this isn't worth it to you, then you have no obligation to keep using it. This is totally risk-free for you to try out and test!

Bonus #2: Totally advanced and custom Web site that will build your list for you on autopilot (a $500 value)

I'm going to build you a custom Web site that will literally attract **hundreds of people** to your site and give you their **personal information**. This site will have what is called a "Facebook opt-in link" so when someone hits the button the Website grabs their real e-mail address from Facebook and it will be added to your list.

But the best part about this Facebook opt-in link is that when someone hits the button, a message pops up on their Facebook page saying they just entered into your program! **Do you know what that means?** This will go viral over Facebook, which is the number-one dominating social media magnet that almost everyone uses!

So How Much Is This?

At this point in my career I charge five hundred dollars an hour for one-on-one consulting. And I have to tell you, I'm phenomenally good at what I do, and it's worth every single penny. I'm not saying that to be arrogant—I'm just stating the truth. I've put in the effort, the time, and the hard work and have invested and continue to invest tens of thousands of dollars over the years to learn what I know and to get to this point where I can look you squarely in the eye and tell you without a doubt that I am worth ten times the investment I charge.

But here's the thing: it took me hundreds of hours to develop the Ultimate Direct Marketing Course for Bar Owners—not just figuring out what worked and what didn't work, but time spent perfecting and refining the system to make it ridiculously simple for bar owners to put into their business the day they get the material.

Like I said, this has taken me hundreds of hours to put together, but let's be conservative and say that it only took me fifty hours. Well, fifty hours of my time at five hundred dollars an hour is twenty-five thousand dollars. ***But you're not going to pay anywhere close to $25K for this.***

Let me ask you, if you just made one thousand dollars more per week to put in your pocket, how much would that be worth to you at the end the of one year? How about if you cut your marketing costs in half and still made an extra one or two thousand in pure profit each week? Seriously, what would that be worth to you?

Imagine that you doubled your sales over the next twelve months. How would that change your business—heck, how would that positively impact your life?

As I told you, my passion is marketing and helping bar owners increase their business and to dominate their competition. My Unique Marketing System will help you do that, and I'm giving you the boldest guarantee—and although I'm not going to give it away, I'm going to price it so no one who is serious about being successful will pass it up. You can get my entire system for just $367, or three investments of $149 each spread out thirty days apart.

$367 for $10,000 or more in sales?

Remember my guarantee? I'm going give you one full year to use this and put ten thousand dollars in your pocket, directly from using my system, plus $1,200 in bonuses. If $367 is too much for you then YOU REALLY NEED THIS!

Go To www.BarOwnerMarketingSystems.com and go to the products tab to purchase.

Bonus Section 2

My Mastermind Coaching and Done-for-You Services

To My Motivated and Determined Bar Owners:

Let me start off by making you a huge promise. If you' read this book and master direct marketing, you will hold in your hand the key to any vault you wish to open. Remove as much from it as you like, and create the life you have always dreamed about.

As I said, that is a huge promise, and perhaps you are not yet convinced. But I'm convinced that if you read the rest of this section and take advantage of the opportunity that is presented to you (if I have openings), "Thank you, Nick" will become your mantra!

Let me prove it to you!

If you know that you should be making more money, working *on* your business and not *in* your business, spending less time at work and more time doing the things you enjoy, then I've got the proven, very different, low-cost marketing secrets that I guarantee **no other bar owner is using in your area**, which will help you dominate your market.

If I have your attention, please keep reading...

Times have changed, and you must be prepared for the worst. The old "customers flowing through your doors" economy is shattered and gone forever! There are few time-honored, reliable business strategies and marketing techniques that continue to have their place—and are even more important than ever. They must be combined with and in sync with the realities of the new economy and the psychology of our customers.

Our customers now have more options than they have ever had. Competition is at its all-time most challenging phase. Are you making yourself stand out from your competition? Are you giving customers a reason to choose you over them without having to discount your prices?

I'm sure you have already seen negative effects to your bottom line. Higher food costs, liquor taxes increasing, etc. Customers are more worried about price than ever before; they are more demanding, they want the world handed to them, and there are fewer customers, which means sales are down altogether.

If this hasn't affected you yet, I'm shocked! But I guarantee you, it's coming.

Why You Should Listen to What I Have to Say

As the owner of Casey's Pub in Loves Park, Illinois, I've gone from the verge of closing down my bar to now being the bar industry's leading authority in developing **low-cost, simple-to-use, effective marketing systems that increase sales and decreases expenses within sixty days.**

I'm now the president and founder of Bar Owner Marketing Systems, but **I'm also a bar owner just like you**. I know what it's like to have slow weeks. I know how it feels to have competition kick your ass! I understand what it's like to deal with some of the world's dumbest people.

This is very important and I'm sure you can relate: I understand how sales reps really work and it's not to help us; it's to collect a commission check from us. They approach us like they are our best friends, tell us they have this special deal for only us, when in reality they are pushing these same deals to our competition. The really bad thing is that **their marketing doesn't even work!** Don't you agree?

We are skeptical people, and we should be! We are in a cash business! We can't trust anyone in this business!

I'm no different then you—except for the fact that I have spent over fifty thousand dollars in the last few years working one-on-one with some of the top small business expert marketers in the country, and I have a passion for marketing and making bar owners more money.

Why You Need an "Automated Customers On Demand" System

An automated marketing system provides consistent cash flow, even during down times. You don't have to lie awake at night wondering how your sales will be the next day. **Having a system like this will give you peace of mind and more freedom to do the things you like.**

Do you know why all these chain bars and restaurants do so well? Why they are popping up all over the country? **Because they have a system for attracting and keeping customers.** They have mastered a system so well that they are able to use expensive advertising to brand themselves—but we small business owners don't have those deep pockets, and that's why we must stick to targeted system if we want more money in our pockets.

Now that I've told you the basics of direct marketing and why mass media is as good as a thief behind your bar, let me tell you an easy way to increase your profits without having to go through the years of learning this the hard way.

It's the most infamous, boldest, brass balls offer and 100-percent risk-free guarantee you will ever get as a bar owner. It's an offer that leaves only *my* time, *my* money, and *my* reputation on the line for *your* business.

My 100-percent Sixty-day Risk-free Money-back Guarantee

My guarantee is that I can take my proven, time-tested, automated marketing systems, which doubled my sales within eight months and increased sales by 23 to 44 percent for multiple bar owners around the country, and put it to work for you in your bar, without any risk or extra work on your part. If you are not 100 percent satisfied with what I have created for you after sixty days, then you don't pay a penny. No questions asked. No note from Mom! No fine line text or hidden clauses.

My Area Exclusive Coaching & Mastermind Program: Why Every Bar Owner Should Have a Mentor or Coach Even if You Have Been in the Business Fifty Years

This may sound unusual for bar owners but if you look at the most successful people in the world—athletes, politicians, businesspeople—they all have relentlessly been molded by a coach for most of their career. For example, Michael Jordan was cut by his high school basketball team before his coach stepped forward and personally mentored him to become the greatest basketball player ever. No one has ever won an Olympic gold medal without a coach. Actors such as John Travolta, Jim Carey, and Tom Cruise all have coaches.

According to *Forbes Magazine*, more and more of the nation's top entrepreneurs and small business owners (and now bar owners) are using coaches and mentors to help achieve new levels of success. These successful people are also outsourcing many of their jobs so they can work less often or focus on more important things in their business.

Regardless of the skills and talents you bring to any profession, achieving success all alone is a grinding, almost hopeless uphill battle. If you're lucky and have already achieved success but are working more than you like, you still haven't achieved freedom from your job—which is where we all want to be. If you have ever felt overwhelmed or stressed out by the seemingly impossible task of building a business that supports your ideal lifestyle, then you will want to read every word I'm about to say.

I started Bar Owner Marketing Systems in 2011. I took on a small number of bar owners and offered them the same exact offer and guarantee I'm offering you right now. I only had one guy drop out (a bowling alley), and the rest are still with me and are extremely impressed with the results.

With that said I've decided to take on another carefully selected handful of bar owners. Because of the demand of my time with each owner and the time I need to spend with my five-year-old son, Leighton, I can't work with everyone, and I am specifically looking to work with bar owners who:

- are motivated and willing to accept a very small change to their business but a big change to their lifestyle and income.
- are willing to invest in themselves and their business.
- are willing to follow a simple, step-by-step action plan (or have a manager willing to do this for you).
- will take responsibility to get things done in a fair amount of time (or have a manager willing to do this for you).

Is this you? If so, you will have the chance to become **one of a chosen few bar owners** from across the country who will have the privilege of learning from, masterminding with, and being coached by me, Nick Fosberg, along with other super successful bar owners.

How would you like to be in a group of fifteen to twenty of the smartest, brightest, and most successful bar owners from all around the country and have access to them as well? Don't you think we all could learn from each other, and then take all that knowledge and dominate our competition?

If you are tired of not getting the results you want and are ready to take your business to the next level, now is your chance. Let me give you an idea of what this program is all about and what impact this could have on your life.

You and I will work hand-in-hand by implementing the revolutionary actions designed to double your income while working less. **Imagine the peace of mind that type of income and freedom will provide!**

I'm talking about developing and teaching the simplest, easiest, and quickest ways to maximize your productivity and balance your life, all without feeling overwhelmed or stressed out. We will work together as a team to define your true goals in life (maybe more money isn't the answer, maybe it's more time off, less stress, one-week vacations every single month). Either way, we will work together to help you design a "life plan" while we continuously tweak and improve every aspect of your personal and professional life to produce multiples of the results you are now obtaining.

My "Double Your Regulars and Profits" Coaching Programs

What are these programs designed to do?

- Bring in at least **one to two hundred new customers** every month. (You can easily do this just by using my party-booking system.)
- Turn new customers into loyal regulars.
- Get your existing customers to come back more often and **spend more money.**
- Create a relationship with your customer through your marketing and make you become a **welcomed marketer** instead of an **unwanted pest** that every other business appears to be.
- Give you a massive edge over your competition by me giving you insider secrets and promotional ideas that are not being done in your area.
- **Make your life easier and stress free** as I create an automated marketing system that runs for you on autopilot to increase your sales and give you the lifestyle you want.

- Give new and existing customers a reason to **choose you** over your competition.

Within one month of starting one of these programs, you're going to come to clearly understand what Napoleon Hill meant when he wrote these memorable words in *Think & Grow Rich*:

"When riches begin to come, they come so quickly, in such great abundance, that one wonders where they have been hiding during all those lean years."

If you haven't read this book get it! Every successful entrepreneur has this book on his or her shelf!

What's included with all of these programs?

- Personal coaching time with me every month to define your quickest ways to maximize your profits without feeling overwhelmed or stressed out. (Just one idea a month can literally put thousands of dollars in your bank account each month.)
- We will create a loyalty program for your bar that is designed to get 75 percent or more of the people who walk through your door to gladly hand over their personal contact information so we can directly market to them, send them offers, and get them coming back more often to spend more money (a $5,000 value).
- We will create a unique, cost-effective marketing plan to get more new customers into your bar using free and extremely low-cost marketing methods **(a $2,500 value)**.
- An **automated** e-mail, text messaging, and direct mail marketing system that runs on autopilot so you don't

have to worry about doing any of the work! **I handle it all so you have more time to do what you want (a $5,000 value).**

- Pre-done sign-up sheets to sign up your customers into your loyalty program **(a $50 value)**.
- A one-page Web site where you can have your employees enter your customers' information so I can then send them irresistible offers through the automated marketing system I create for you **(a $100 value)**.
- A two-page Web site designed to capture people's information and get them into your marketing funnel. This site will include all the social media widgets and allow people to spread your site like a wildfire all over the Internet and Facebook. This site alone will give you a huge advantage over you competition **(a $750 value)**.
- **My Ultimate Direct Marketing Course for Bar Owners**. You will get my complete course with audio CDs and a CD with all my marketing materials that you can copy. All you have to do is add in your information and your logo! This course will give you everything you need as a reference anytime you are looking for a new idea **(a $367 value).**

Discover Why a Mastermind Group and a Coach Are the TRUE Secrets of Success

My coaching program incorporates the most powerful, state-of-the-art teaching and learning methods available to the bar industry, including allowing you to tap into the power of the "mastermind." The power of a mastermind is insanely valuable!

Napoleon Hill, author of *Think and Grow Rich*, made this discovery after years of studying the world's richest and most successful people: "You need brains besides your own." That is step nine to riches in his classic book *Belonging to a Mastermind Group*.

Besides allowing you to tap into the power of the mastermind you will discover the extraordinary benefits of having your own personal coach. If the world's most successful athletes attribute much of their success to having a great coach, **shouldn't you tap into this success secret and start working with your own coach to help you achieve your business and personal goals as well?** Like I said, I wouldn't be where I'm at today if it weren't for my coaches and mentors. I became very successful. and I still to this day gladly invest with them to stay on top of my competition and work on my goals.

What if the only thing preventing you from finally achieving what you really want out of life is not having a coach?

Having a coach eliminates any frustration you have if you feel stuck and can't decide what to do. If you have questions, they are answered. If you need a "kick in the ass" to get motivated, you've got it! I still to this day get "kicks in the ass" from my coaches—just not as many as I used to because over time **I've developed a system for getting the most important things done that make me the most amount of money in the shortest amount of time. I will do the same for you!**

I will push you or even your manager to test your limits and achieve far more than you ever thought you were capable of achieving. I'll be there to guide you and help you ever bit of the way.

Can You Put a Price on Success?

Obviously there is a monthly investment for my time and guidance—and like I stated before **I'm giving you sixty days risk free to work with me** (only if you get your application in fast enough and are accepted into one of the programs). If you are not happy with the results after sixty days, **I will refund 100 percent of your money, no questions asked.**

I haven't had one refund yet, and this is because I know who is motivated and willing to partner with me and listen. I've worked with lazy bar owners, and I have let them go and returned their money. If certain guidelines are not done in thirty days, I let them go because this shows me who is serious and who isn't.

What Are the Prices?

The lower-end package of my program is extremely affordable, but the high-end package is not cheap. I'll make no apologies for that. Of course, my own education and expertise has not come cheap either. Like I've said, I've invested over fifty thousand dollars in coaching and training, and I continue to spend another twenty-five thousand year after year. Honestly, you can't put a price on the value that you will get in return. You will stretch higher, work wiser, and undergo transformation at a level you can't begin to imagine yet.

In the end, your initial investment of time and money will seem absolutely nil in comparison to the wealth you'll receive—both in swelling your bank account and in the value of your fresh ideas and new, stress-free lifestyle.

Remember, I will be evaluating applications on a first-come, first-served basis. Once I reach my limit of new candidates who fully qualify for these special mastermind coaching programs, I will close the doors and no additional applications will be accepted. If you are serious about maximizing your income, working less, and finally getting to where you "really" want to be, take the next step and get the application in today! Don't procrastinate like everyone else.

How to Get Your Application in Today

- Go To www.BarOwnerMarketingSystems.com/Application and fill it out online.
- Call 815 669 0780 and leave a message with your information. My receptionist will get one off to you right away.
- E-mail me at Nickfosberg@gmail.com and I will e-mail you an application.

Free 20 Minute Marketing Consultation $250 Value

Thank You For Investing In My Book

My goal is to help bar owners with their most profitable & important job, MARKETING! But the truth is most bar restaurant owners are clueless about how to market their bar, what kinds of media's to use, who to target, what message to use, how to define the best customer to go after, and how to turn these new customers into loyal regulars.

The way the consultation will works is I will send you a list of 10-15 questions about your bar & competition. I will then create a strategic marketing plan for you that fits your budget.

There are only 3 outcomes from this call. You will take my advice and do it yourself and increase your profits, you will want to hire me to do it all for you so you can get results quickly, or you will do nothing with it at all.

How To Set Up Consultation

Go to www.BarOwnerMarketingSystems.com and go to the contact tab and leave a message there that you bought the book and want your free consultation.

Call **815-669-0780**, please leave a detailed message if receptionist does not answer

I can guarantee the call to be within 3 weeks of scheduling, but I can't guarantee that I can take you on as a private client, if you feel that's what you need. I only work with a small handful of bar owners at a time. I can add you to a waiting list if there is one at that time.

Bonus Report

"The Bar Restaurant Owner's Who Don't Continue To Change & Keep Up With Today's Ever Changing Tech World Are The One's Who Are Losing Profits & Falling Behind Their Competition....

Discover How To Increase Your Profits & Put Your Entire Business In The Palm Of Thousands Of Customers Hands Every Day Using Today's Most Powerful Marketing Media Ever Invented.

Bar Restaurant Owners, Who Don't Even Know How To Turn On A Computer, Are Reporting Rising Profits Within 31 Days

By Nick Fosberg
The Bar Restaurant's Leading Marketing Authority

Welcome to the digital world. Whether you like it or not, technology is here to stay and it's growing at rapid speeds. Even if you hate technology or don't want to learn about technology, this report is worth reading because you will discover what the future holds for your business, your customers, and your success.

As a bar or restaurant owner your job isn't to know all the tech stuff so don't let this report scare you. Your main focus needs to be marketing because that is what drives customers into your bar. Marketing is the most important & profitable job you have. What I'm here to tell you is how to use a mobile app as a all in one marketing solution and how to turn new customers into raving fans about your business.

How would you like to have a simple, low cost, all in one marketing solution that:

- does 10-15 different marketing strategies that attracts currents customers and new customers like a magnet
- keeps customers up to date on new events every day at the palm of their hands
- gets customers to spread the word about your bar in ways word of mouth could never do
- makes all this happen automatically for a fraction of the cost of what you are spending on marketing now
- connects with your customers in a way that no other marketing media has ever done before

The internet, cell phones, I Pad's, Navigation Systems, E-mail, Text Messaging, etc, etc, are now controlling almost everyone on this planet. There is no denying that. Pretty soon you will be able to have your I phone call in sick for you using your mothers voice and when it hangs up a automated fax will go out to your boss with her signature.

What's To Come In 2015

According to the International Data Corporation, by 2015, more people will be accessing the web through mobile devices than through PC's. So the question for you is....

What are you doing to take advantage of that momentum? Are you going to sit on the band wagon or are you going to be aggressive and profit from this evolution that has hit your customers like a time bomb.

Bar restaurant owners now need to start looking at technology as their primary solution for bringing in new customers. Why? That's the way the world has shifted. People have satellite radio, the newspaper is on their cell phone, you tube is on their I pad, etc, etc.. Newspaper, Tv, Radio, and any other kind of advertising you used in the past is dead. Plus it's just too damn expensive!!

The Only Way You Need To Market Your Bar is Through E-mail, Texting, Social Media, & Direct Mail.

Why? It inexpensive, it's reliable, it's the most direct advertising you can do, and it's the most profitable. What I have to share with you today has all 5 components built into one simple package

My goal is for this report to open your eyes to what is to come and what is **guaranteed to happen.** If you don't see the **BIG** opportunity here today...... you will after every one of your competitors gets to it first.

"But I Don't Understand Technology" "I Don't Want To Learn How To Use This"

I understand completely! Don't worry. I'm going to explain to you how easy it is to set all this up and how you can have it all set up for you and maintained for you on a monthly basis. Like I said, if us bar owners tried to do everything in our business, we would have no life, no fun, and be stressed out all the time. **That's why we hire people to do the things we don't want to do!!**

All In One Marketing Solution

Let me introduce to you, a marketing tool that is a all in one marketing system. A marketing tool that has never been so powerful. A marketing tool that is so inexpensive that with the power and out reach it has to your customers, it could possibly eliminate 67% percentage of your marketing expenses and get you 3 to 4 times a better response rate.

The Ultimate "Mobile App" For Bar Restaurant Owners

What is a app? A app is pretty much a piece of software that is installed on your smart phone or on your I pad that has more power & functions than our first spaceship. Yea crazy to think of it like that but it's true.

Here are a few things you can have in your app and I will go over more in detail on these in a little bit.

- Your menu
- Your social media sites
- Your website
- Your specials and up coming events
- Directions to your business through map quest
- Incentive / Loyalty program that is designed to capture customers contact information so you can continue to send them offers from text, email, and direct mail

- A "tell a friend" feature that allows people to spread your app to the world
- Simple "Call" feature. They just click it and it calls you
- A suggestion feature so people can tell you what they like, don't like, and suggestions on new specials and promotions
- Plus much much more

Statistics That Will Blow Your Mind

1 & 4 Adults Now Use Mobile Apps by by Lauren Indvik

A new study from the Pew Internet Project illustrates just how rapidly consumers are embracing applications on their mobile devices.

Of the 82% of U.S. adults who are now active cellphone users, 43% now have apps on their phones, and more than two-thirds of them use those apps regularly. In other words, 24% of the U.S. adult population actively uses apps, the study estimates.

Of the 82% Americans using mobile devices, nearly one-third of them have downloaded apps, and 13% said they have paid for one or more of those apps. More than half of those who said they had downloaded an app claimed they had done so within the last 30 days, and one-third had in the last week.

Of those who have downloaded apps, nearly 2 in 3 said they use their apps daily, and 1 in 4 use their apps for more than 30 minutes per day. Most (71%) use their apps alone, while roughly half use them while waiting for someone or something, or while at work. Another 36% use their apps while commuting (which happens to be when I use apps most heavily).

"Mobile Marketing Is The Most Powerful Advertising Media Ever Invented"
New York Times

Did You Know.....

1. **That mobile web growth is happening *4 times* as fast as the speed of the internet**
2. ***One out of every 7 minutes* media consumption takes place on mobile**
3. **There are over 5,000 different mobile devices that can access the mobile web**

What Does This Mean To You & Your Future?

If you want to keep customers or increase your customer base, a mobile app is not a question. It's mandatory! It's not one of the most affordable & profitable marketing media's you could have. It is the most affordable & profitable media you could have.

Stats show that 2 in 3 people who use apps use them daily. How would you like your customers looking at your specials, looking at your pictures, spreading the word about your business to their friends for you, giving you suggestions on what they would like as special, telling you different promotions they would like, **EVERY SINGLE DAY?**

It's not a question of if you will ever get an app for your bar. It's when are you going to get an app. Remember when texting services hit our industry? You might have sat on the sideline for a while but eventually you got it because you saw how every one of your customers used texting.....**Well here you are again!!**

The "5" Most Important Features Of Your App That You Must Have To Increase Sales, Double Your Loyal Regulars, And Stay On Top Of Your Competition.

#1 Loyalty Program / Incentive Program

Whether you have a loyalty program right now or you don't, this is the most important feature and strategy you could do.

In your app you must have a loyalty program or Incentive Program. Why? Because it's designed to collect people's information so you can continue to market to them.

What is so powerful about this is people are taking the time to fill out the form in order to receive your offers and discounts. There is **NOBODY** else or any other type of advertising you can do that is more profitable then to marketing to people who **WANT** to hear from you!

This is direct marketing! ***This is what every bar owner needs to be doing if they want to turn new customers into loyal regulars and get their existing customers to come back more often to fill their registers with cash!!***

Collecting their email address, cell phone number, and mailing address are the most important things you need to be collecting. A loyalty program or incentive program can do that for you and by having this in your app, it does everything automatically. Most bar restaurant owners don't do this because of the organization it takes and because they are LAZY. They wonder why their sales are down and wonder why they can't get new business!! Having an app and doing everything you are reading in this report will solve that problem.

#2 Tell A Friend Feature

The tell a friend feature allows your app users to spread the word about your app through facebook, twitter, email, etc, etc. Remember, your app is to provide all your specials, upcoming events, details about your bar / restaurant, and menu.

So if you can get your app users spreading this for you, you're putting your business, your specials, and your events in front of thousands of people for free. Usually you have to spend hundreds if not thousands of dollars to do this through radio, tv, and newspaper advertising....**Not ANYMORE!**

3 Your Social Media Sites

We all know how social media has taken over. There are now over 800 million people on facebook and millions of tweets being tweeted every single day. Like it or not but this is how people are now communicating. This is what people **LIKE** and the way they **WANT** to communicate. So shouldn't you adapt to get a better response from your marketing????

Having twitter, facebook, yelp, etc, etc on your app allows your customers to get even more information about you. It allows them to interact with you as well. This is what social media is based on. Connecting and interacting with people.

I'm sure you are using social media for your marketing right? Most bar restaurants are and most are not seeing results or anything from it. There are different strategies and techniques that must be applied.

Just putting your special out there isn't going to do a whole lot for you. You need to get people interacting with you and you need ways to capture their personal information so you can continue to market to them. Again...The people who give you their personal contact information are the most profitable people you could ever market to...So why market to anyone else?

I'm not going to get into social media marketing but it is powerful if used correctly and if this is something you would like to get more answers on, be sure to get my contact from the end of this report to contact me.

#4 Read Now Feature

If you want to get the most out of your app you must follow this step by step. I saved this for last because it applies to everything else that I just talked about.

You need a Read Now button that thanks them for downloading the app and that tells them how to get the most value from it. You will want to tell them what to do step by step.

Every app I set up for my private coaching clients the read me now page goes like this...

==================================

Thanks for download "Billy Bob's Bar App". My name is Billy Bob (you will have a picture of yourself next to all this to introduce yourself) and I'm the owner. I want you to take 1 minute to read this so you get the best value from this app. I'm not your usual bar / restaurant owner. I tend to give back more than I should but I do it because I believe that the more you give back the better and more respected customers you will have.

To get the most out of this app please read below...

#1 Click The Vip Button

This will allow you to get 50% off offers to free dinners to invites to our loyalty parties. Just add your phone number and hit submit and every so often you will get a text with specials and offers. I don't send 3-4 texts a week like most places so don't worry about that. I only send about one a week with offers that you won't get anywhere els

#2 Click The Loyalty Button

This will get you in our loyalty program. Right when you sign up you get a gift card sent ot your house, plus you will get $15 a moth in free gift cards...Yes $15 every month! $180 a year! I'm also going to give you 10% off your tabs every time you come in. Tell me what other bar / restaurant is doing this for their customers

#3 Tell A Friend

I hate to ask for favors but I'm going to ask anyways. For me giving you all these discounts and $180 a year in free gift cards, would you mind sharing this app with your friends and family so they can get the same deals? Don't you think they would be mad if you didn't share this?

This is how easy this is. Everyone uses facebook, wouldn't you agree? Well there is a feature on here titled "Tell A Friend" All you have to do is click it and then click the facebook link and the app will automatically appear on your facebook page! You don't even have to write any text or anything, it just automatically happens! If you could do this for me I would really appreciate it.

Thanks again for downloading the app and if you think I could add any other features, I'm open for suggestions.

==================================

If you want to get the most out of your app, you must tell the exactly what to do and how to do it. You need to direct them and hold their hand like you are their mother.

I'm Now Educated On Why I Need A Mobile App. Now What??

If you are this far into the report then you must agree that mobile apps are the wave of the future for the bar restaurant industry. There is no denying that. The facts and studies alone easily prove that. With that said are you going sit and wait or be aggressive and start profiting from this **ALL IN ONE MARKETING SOLUTION**?

I've told you about just a few of the most important marketing features that will literally spread your business across the internet to thousands of people in your area. There is no other marketing media that 2 of out 3 people will look at your content or your offers every single day!! People are addicted to their phones and you need real estate in the palm of their hands.

You Won't Get This Anywhere Else, Guaranteed!!

There are multiple mobile app companies that you can research to see who has the best prices & features. All you need to do is google "mobile apps" on your computer and you will find thousands of places to go. I encourage you to do so ***but I'm going to give you a solution that no other company can give for you for the same price that you will get anywhere else.***

I've partnered with a mobile marketing company that provides mobile apps & texting services. Together, we have created a mobile app marketing program that no other company can compare to because this program includes the **key to your success with mobile app marketing.**

That Key Is Guidance, Support, & Marketing Expertise

Anybody can have a app! But not everyone knows how to maximize it's power.

Every company out there can create a mobile app for you, but where do you go from there? Every company can provide a website for you, but where do you go from there. They key to success in any business is **MARKETING!** The truth is most bar restaurants owners are clueless about marketing. I know this because I talk to over 100 bar/restaurant owners a month about marketing and solving their problems.

What we are going to do for you is create your app for you with the most up to date technology & features designed for bar restaurant owners, but I'm also going to spend personal time on the phone with you to tell you how to..

1. Get 100 people or more to download your app on your first day
2. **Use the tell a friend feature to get 500 or more people to download your app per month (just think how your business will grow when you have**

3,000-5,000 people looking at your app, specials, promotions, facebook page every single day)

3. Turn new customers into loyal regulars
4. How to have your app **paid for by another company**
5. How to cut your marketing costs in half
6. Plus I will also give you some of my **most valuable marketing insider secrets** that will allow you to dominate your competition.

Yes, you can get a mobile app from thousands of companies out there but you won't get what **REALLY MATTERS**, and that is a marketing plan to actually make your mobile app **Effective and Profitable.**

Let me ask you this, and like I said I encourage you to look at all the other options you have available, would you rather get a mobile app through a company who knows nothing about bar restaurant marketing or go through a company who has a bar restaurant marketing expert on their side who **personally works with their clients and tells them exactly what to do and how to do it**?

What All Comes With Your Mobile App?

You are going to get all the 5 features I talked about earlier plus many more

1. **Find Us Feature-** This allows people who don't know where your bar or restaurant is to find you easily through google maps.
2. **Deals & Promotions-** This will allow you to post all your daily specials and events coming up for weeks or even months

3. **Custom Page-** You can even create custom pages that you may already have on the web and apply them to your app
4. **Video's-** You can post any kind of video that you want straight from YOU TUBE!
5. **Menu-** Apply your menu to your app so people know what you have to offer
6. **Text Alerts-** If you have text messaging you can have a feature to get more people into your data base with the touch of a button. (This is a great way to build your mobile marketing)
7. **Facebook & Twitter-** You can have all your facebook and twitter accounts hooked right up into one spot so your mobile app users never miss a special or promo
8. **Contact Page-** This allows people to contact you about whatever it is they want by email or by phone.
9. **Suggestion Feature-** You can use this to get suggestions about specials, promotions, food items, etc, etc... The goal to your business is to provide customers with what they want.....Well find out what they want and give it to them!!!
10. **Loyalty Feature-** This is the smartest thing you can do. It's 7-10 more profitable to market to people who sign up to get offers from you. This allows you to capture full contact information so you can send emails, texts, and direct mail to them

There are so many other features that you can have but these are the top 10, plus the other 5 "Must Have Features" I mentioned earlier in the report.

Do you see why I call this a "All In One Marketing Solution"? This one app takes care of everything you need to stay in contact with your customers and it's ***the number one way to capture people's information and get them into your marketing funnel.***

So How Much Is It?

We have created 3 different very affordable packages for you to choose from plus a couple extra bonuses that go along with them that you won't get with any other company.

Silver Package $299 Set Up / $99 Month

The silver package is a one time fee of $299 which includes creating unlimited pages for your mobile app and $99 per month which includes the done for you mobile app service where we handle 100% of all your changes. All you need to do is give us a 24 hour notice!

Some companies only allow your app to be on certain mobile devices such as only iphone or only android. The mobile app we create for you will be able to be downloaded to any mobile device there is. This is another huge benefit because no matter what everyone can download your business straight to their phone.

Here's the big bonus ($250 Value)

The silver package includes all the viral marketing features, but you are also going to get a 20 minute call with me so I can give you a step by step system to get hundreds of people to get your app within the first few days. This one phone call with me will literally put thousands of extra dollars in your pockets this year.

Gold Package $299 Set Up / $199 A month

This includes everything above plus **UNLIMITED TEXTING**. Most companies will charge you anywhere from .02 cents to .04 cents per message. If you have a list of 3,000 people (which is easy to have if you follow my simple marketing plan to do it) and if you are getting charged .02 cents per message times 2 texts per week, your looking at 12,000 total texts, which would cost you $240 a month....and that's without the app!

Do you have texting now? How much are you paying? Even if you don't want the app (not sure why your wouldn't), but this company also provides unlimited texting for only $99 per month. You won't find this deal anywhere else. I use the same service for my bar and so do all my private coaching clients.

Platinum Package $399 Set Up / $275 A Month

Are really looking for a simple & easy customers on demand system? **Then this is exactly what you need.** If you could only spend $275 on marketing and get better results than what you are getting now, how would that make you feel?

If you are not marketing at all because you haven't seen a return on your marketing dollars, I suggest you get over that right now and start using **WHAT WORKS...** Tv, Radio, Newspaper, Money Mailers, and any other large distribution is no longer the answer.

The Platinum Package includes the gold & silver package plus a proven guaranteed to work loyalty program that is designed to turn new customers into loyal regulars.

This program is the same exact one I create for all my private coaching clients. This also includes a lead capture website that will literally put hundreds of people into your database within just 3-5 weeks by using **my secret marketing strategies that only my private clients get access to.**

I also include the Facebook opt in sign up form on your web pages for you, which means when someone clicks the "Sign Up With Facebook" tab on your site a message pops up on **THEIR** facebook page saying they **just signed up for your program and tells people to click the link attached to do the same thing.**

Do you know what this does?

Makes your program go viral, just like the tell a friend feature for the app. ***When you combine these two things together, you have a marketing power house on steroids!***

My proven loyalty program / incentive program is what you need to turn new customers into loyal regulars and get your existing customers to come back more often. The hardest part of marketing is staying organized and being efficient. How would you like to have 90% of you marketing done for you? That's what this package is all about!

But Loyalty Programs Don't Work!?!?!?!?

If I had a dollar for every bar owner who has told me this I wouldn't be writing this report right now. The only reason they don't work is because you can't get anyone to sign up and the reason for that is **your not making a strong enough offer.** Why the hell should anyone give you their personal contact information if they are not getting something valuable in return?

The other reason they might not work is because of poor follow up. You might get people in, but your not using the right ways to get them back in to spend more money. The key to this is a great follow up campaign using direct mail, texting, and e-mail.

I create automated follow up systems for all my clients and I can help you create the same exact thing when you get the platinum package.

"This All Sounds Great But I Don't Understand Technology & Don't Have The Drive To Put This To Work In My Business"

I understand and this is one of the main reasons I started working with bar owners outside my area. Technology is confusing. Most bar owners just want everything done for them. We don't want to learn anything new. We just want money being stuffed in our registers while we are golfing, vacationing, boating, or what ever else it is we like to do. So I created multiple done for you programs where I take the hard work off bar owners shoulders and do the work for them. Makes life 10 times easier!

Every program that I have explained in this report doesn't require you to learn anything at all! We set everything up for you plus I tell you (or your manager who is in charge of your marketing) how to utilize this **ALL IN**

<u>ONE MARKETING SOLUTION</u> so you get everything you need out of it to make your business more profitable.

Like I stated before, every other company out there is going to create this for you, but none of them are going to tell you how to make it effective. They just take your money and run. I'm actually going to give 10-15 ways to get thousands of people to have your business in the palm of their hands every day.

How Do I Invest In My Business & Take Advantage Of The Most Powerful Marketing System In The World

Go to www.BarRestaurantMobileMarketing.com and select the package that fits your needs or call 815-669-0780 for more information

Made in the USA
San Bernardino, CA
11 February 2016